TeamMates

TeamMates

BUILDING YOUR MARRIAGE TO COMPLETE, NOT COMPETE

Bob and Yvonne Turnbull

Beacon Hill Press of Kansas City
Kansas City, Missouri

Copyright 1998
by Beacon Hill Press of Kansas City

ISBN 083-411-7177

Printed in the
United States of America

Cover Design: Paul Franitza
Cover Photo: FPG

Library of Congress Cataloging-in-Publication Data
Turnbull, Bob, 1936-
    TeamMates : building your marriage to complete, not compete / Bob and Yvonne Turnbull.
        p.   cm.
    ISBN 0-8341-1717-7 (pbk.)
    1. Spouses—Religious life. 2. Marriage—Religious aspects—Christianity. I. Turnbull, Yvonne. II. Title.
BV4596.M3T87   1998
248.8'44—DC21
                                                                98-27231
                                                                    CIP

10   9   8   7   6   5   4   3   2   1

This book is dedicated to Robert and Misti Turnbull, our beloved son and daughter-in-law. We pray God's richest blessing on their journey of becoming TeamMates.

We also dedicate this book to our new grandson, Jackson Dean Turnbull, and we pray that someday he will experience the joyful adventure of a Christian marriage and being a TeamMate.

Contents

Foreword

My husband, Andy, and I have enjoyed and been blessed by the friendship of Bob and Yvonne Turnbull for many, many years. This is a couple who love each other, love God, and live life to the fullest. As you read this book you will feel like you know them well.

You'll also see yourself in these pages. Whether your marriage is in trouble and needs fixing or just needs a little fine-tuning, you'll appreciate the Turnbulls' effective and encouraging way of challenging us all to continue to grow and deepen our commitments to each other.

My husband likes to say that "marriage takes three" . . . you, God, and your partner. This book will give you the tools you need to build a deeply satisfying and lasting marriage. *TeamMates* is user-friendly, practical, and effective. A great opportunity to be sure your marriage is all God intends for it to be.

Terry Meeuwsen
Cohost of *The 700 Club*

Introduction

*There is no more lovely, friendly and charming
relationship, communion or company than
a good marriage.*
—Martin Luther

Jessica was already seated on the airplane when Yvonne took
her place in the seat next to her. She was one of the many children that we see traveling alone on planes every week. She was
headed back to her mother and stepfather after spending a
weekend with her father, stepmother, and new baby brother. Before the plane took off, a conversation between Jessica and
Yvonne began.

As the conversation progressed, Yvonne became aware this
was a sad little girl on the inside with a smile on the outside.
Soon she told how she hated to fly back and forth to visit her
dad. All she wanted was to have her mom and dad back together. She revealed that she was getting mixed up about her new
brother. She asked, "Is he my real brother, half-brother, or step-
brother?" She sighed, then looked at Yvonne and said, "Life is
so complicated."

"Complicated." A big word for a little girl, and already she
not only knows its meaning but is experiencing it.

This is why we've written this book—to help keep families
together. For the past 14 years we've traveled the United States
and Canada and presented our marriage and family seminars,
and we've found so many couples looking for answers for their
marriage. Many don't have the background or knowledge of
what it takes to make a marriage work. Many are lacking any
hope that there can be answers for them. Our desire with *Team-
Mates* is to renew that hope.

There are many ways to read this book, but we suggest that
the best way is for a husband and wife to read it together. You
might want to take turns reading pages or chapters out loud to

each other. Read one chapter a week. Don't forget to hit your personal pause button so you can give serious reflection and discuss the team-building questions and action steps you'll find at the end of each chapter. These will help strengthen your communication.

Another way to maximize *TeamMates* is to consider using it in a group discussion, such as a Sunday School class or a home group study. Several couples can read a chapter and then discuss the questions together. It can be helpful to hear that other couples have the same struggles and the same successes.

Our prayer is that our Lord Jesus Christ will touch your heart, mind, and soul in a very special way as you read each chapter.

Building Block No. 1

Unity

1

This Is Living Happily Ever After?

TEAM BUILDING GOD'S WAY

Love does not consist in gazing at each other,
but in looking outward together in the same direction.
—Antoine DeSaint-Exupery

When people ask us where we met, Bob always answers with "I met Yvonne when she was working a hotel in Waikiki."

Eyebrows go up, so Yvonne quickly adds, "That sounds great, Dear. Now are you going to tell them what you mean by that?"

Bob: *I was walking down the hallway in the Reef Towers Hotel in Hawaii, en route to my office at the Waikiki Beach chaplaincy. I always passed by a travel agency office and would automatically look in and wave to the staff. The owner, a friend of mine, was a man, but his staff were all local Hawaii-born females, each with beautiful long black hair, just like you'd see on "Hawaii 5-0" and "Magnum, P.I." But one day as I walked and waved, out of the corner of my eye I noticed there was this blond in the midst of the black-haired girls. So I said to my thongs, "Halt. Back up." They reversed themselves until I was able to take that famous second look. Sure enough, there she was, standing in the middle of the room, very animated and looking mighty good. Little did I know that someday this bubbly blond would become my wife. Since my eyes noticed this new talent in town, I quickly seized the mo-*

ment to snake—I mean ease—my way into the room to extend the friendly aloha spirit.

Yvonne: *After graduating from Washington State University and then doing some postgrad work at the University of Washington, I needed some rest and relaxation. So I went to Hawaii for a few weeks, which stretched into a few months. Being a new Christian, I heard about a worship service on the beach at the Hilton Hawaiian Village every Sunday morning. It was well known on Oahu as "Sun and Soul Talk." That sounded like my style of worship, so I went one Sunday morning to hear the Waikiki Beach chaplain speak. I had heard so much about him, but on the Sunday I attended he was speaking on the mainland. The service was nice, but I didn't return. When I noticed this hunk walk into my office that day, and when he introduced himself to me, I realized this was the man I had gone to hear at the beach, and after looking at him, I thought, "All right—I'm definitely going back to the beach service!"*

Bob: *I wanted to get to know her but didn't want to get too pushy by asking for a date since I had known her for only 30 seconds. So I did the safe thing. I invited her to come to the beach service the next Sunday. She agreed.*

Yvonne: *I was hoping I would get to see him again, so when he invited me to the beach service I was happy to accept. I wasn't even thinking that I was a "cheap date"—only that I would get to know him better. The next Sunday I showed up with a beach towel, bathing suit, and sunglasses, and that was the start of many cheap dates to the beach services and Bible studies for the next three years.*

That's right. We got married a full three years after that first meeting. The long wait was mainly because neither of us was quite sure we were ready for that big step of marriage. Second, half of each year Bob traveled the mainland speaking, so it took us longer to build our relationship than if he had remained in Hawaii day in and day out.

The special day finally arrived, and we were both eager to say our "I dos." Our wedding took place in a garden setting in beautiful Manoa Valley, against the mountains, complete with a mist falling upon the small gathering of family and friends.

Yvonne was a nervous bride for more than the usual reasons. Bob had to fly into Hawaii in time for the wedding, and he was starting his journey to the wedding from Israel. If you know anything about international flights, you are well aware that there can be many delays for a variety of reasons. Bob had to fly from Israel to Rome to New York to Los Angeles to Honolulu and get there by 3:00 for a 5:00 wedding. Would that make *you* nervous?

Bob's plane arrived in Honolulu at 3:15. The wedding started on time, and Mr. and Mrs. Bob Turnbull IV were united in Christ and ready to start an adventure we never would have dreamed of or imagined. Our "happily ever after" marriage!

A Fairy-Tale Marriage?

Yvonne: *My first thought when awaking the morning of our wedding day was "This is a dream come true." I had found a man who would fulfill all my needs for love and attention. He would be so eager to rush home to me every night and spend all his time just talking to and listening to me. He would surprise me with little gifts and things he had done for me. We would keep the romance fires flaming for the rest of our married life.*

Bob: *Wow—I'm getting a wife. A wife created by God to meet my needs. I'll be the head of the home. She'll be the heart. I'll be the leader, and she'll be the submissive "little woman." What more could I want? This'll be great—just great!*

Yvonne: *I read all the fairy tales as a young girl, and evidently I believed the one about Prince Charming carrying his princess off to his castle. The problem was that no one told me that besides picking up after him I was going to have to clean up after his horse. The reality check for me came as soon as our honeymoon. It began with my husband going back to work Sunday morning, after a Friday wedding, to speak at the beach service. It wasn't just that the length of the honeymoon was so short. It was that I hardly spent any time with him. He slept most of the honeymoon because he was so exhausted from having just returned from his lengthy trip to Israel. Then he spent most of the hours he was awake working on his Sunday message.*

Bob: *I assumed Yvonne knew I would be tired from my lengthy trip and that I had only a short time to get my Sunday message prepared. I realized this was a quickie honeymoon and not the ideal circumstances, but I assumed she would understand and would overlook it.*

Yvonne: *That weekend I was already asking, "Hey—what happened to the long hours of talking, cuddling, and romancing?" I found* *this reality was the beginning of a pattern for many years in our marriage. I discovered early that work was what seemed to capture most of his time and effort. I always felt as if I got the leftovers. So to get his attention, guess what I started doing. That's right—nagging, by saying things like "How come it seems you don't want to talk to me?" "How come everyone else's needs seem so much more important than mine?"*

Bob: *I would shrug her off with inane comments like "Honey, just hang in there. I'm really involved doing God's work, and you know that. I'll spend time with you on my day off."*

Yvonne: *Guess what usually happened on his day off. Ministry emergencies that he just had to attend to, of course. Other married members of the Waikiki Beach chaplaincy spent time together on their days off, but not my Bob. It was then that I began to feel that he was married to the ministry more than to me. But he was doing God's work, so who was I to speak against that? Thus, in order not to feel the pain of loneliness and rejection, I decided to become very busy. I would definitely stay married, because neither of us would consider divorce as an option, but I started living a double life. By that I mean that Bob and I remained a married couple, but I also started a life for myself apart from Bob. I put my energies into many activities, either alone or with my girlfriends. I figured that since he was busy I would be busy too.*

Both of us desired to be close to each other. We just didn't know how. It seemed everything we tried either just didn't click or completely backfired. We were agonizingly and slowly drifting farther apart. This went on for years. No one told us that it's not easy to live happily ever after.

As with many other couples, numerous circumstances entered in that put more stress on an already-stressed marriage. We were moving nearly every two years of our married life. Some of the moves took us completely across the country. Others were just a matter of blocks away. Most were related to job opportunities, while others were because the rental houses we were in were either sold or foreclosed on. We looked forward to some of the moves. Some we did not—like the two cross-country ones we did at Christmastime.

In the midst of all of this, our finances were stretched to the edge. Matters worsened once when we were in California and we both lost our jobs on the same day. We were cohosting a

Monday-through-Friday radio show, and when the new management took over they fired everyone working at the station. In radio parlance, that's called "The Friday Massacre." Instead of working together as a team during those stress-filled times, we battled each other. It seemed that every time we tried to talk to each other, the result would be an argument. Our marriage started as an *ideal* but then became an *ordeal* that bottomed out as a *raw* deal. What we needed was a *new* deal.

The God of Hope Intervened

Yvonne: *We were at our lowest point. I remember one afternoon when I was, as usual, home alone. I sat on the couch and burst into tears. Deep tears. I was so lonely and hurt. I cried out, "Dear God, we need Your intervention. We need Your help. We need hope that our marriage can and will be different."*

Bob: *As Yvonne was crying and praying, I was just a few blocks away from home, just moments from pulling into the driveway. I was depressed and frustrated and echoed a similar prayer to God. I remember almost shouting, "God, please give us a verse of hope that we can cling to so we can start rebuilding our marriage!" It was then the Lord pulled up a verse from my memory that I hadn't used in years. Rom. 15:13 — "May the God of hope fill you with all joy and peace as you trust in him, so that you may overflow with hope by the power of the Holy Spirit."*

Yvonne: *Bob rushed into the room, looked at me, dropped to his knees in front of me, and said, "Honey, Romans 15:13. We need to believe it, claim it, and apply it." He quoted it to me and added, "We have little hope, joy, or peace in our marriage, because, though we're Christians, we're trying to make this marriage work in our own strength. We're not trusting—really trusting—in God. Our marriage needs to overflow with hope by the power of the Holy Spirit, who lives in us. That can happen. Let's do it."*

God Did Have a New Deal for Us!

God met us at our lowest point as we cried out to Him for help, and on that very day He started to rebuild and renew our marriage. We realized we had been trying to set up and handle our marriage just by ourselves, thinking we had a better plan than God's plan for a Christian marriage. We finally understood the reality written in Ps. 127:1: "Unless the LORD builds the house, its builders labor in vain." For too long we had labored in vain. We were ready for a new plan by the Creator of marriage.

Our first step in making a change in our marriage came with the knowledge that God put us together as a *team*. When we read or hear the word "team," we often think of great sports teams like the Broncos, Packers, Dodgers, Braves, Lakers, or Bulls. Or the music team of Rodgers and Hammerstein, who created incredible musical notes and lyrics. Or the comedy teams of Martin and Lewis, Abbott and Costello, Burns and Allen.

But the team we can learn the most from is the very first marriage team. The team of Adam and Eve. That story begins in the Garden of Eden.

As the narrative unfolds, we find Adam just created and placed by God in the garden, followed by the animals. God then deemed Adam the zookeeper of the garden. To do his job well, he knew he had to call them something other than "Hey, you!" He needed to give each type of animal a name.

In the midst of this job he came to the realization that there was no one just like him. He was beginning to feel pretty lonely. Here he was in this perfect environment. He didn't have to pull weeds (there weren't any), didn't have to mow the lawn. He had a cushy job playing basketball with the giraffes, training the hippos how to be NFL down linemen, doing wind sprints with the cheetahs—play time all day long. There wasn't anybody around telling him to "pick up your stuff." Plus he had the God of the universe as a companion. Yet he was still lonely; he desired to have a companion more like him, someone he could talk to face-to-face, someone he could walk beside.

God knew this would happen, of course. He was just waiting for Adam to catch on. In Gen. 2:18 He declared, "It is not good for the man to be alone." Since the loneliness wasn't good, He prepared to take care of it by providing Adam with a creation similar to, yet different from, him. That creation would be a complement to Adam's personality, to his manhood.

In verses 21 and 22 of Genesis 2 we read that the Lord God put Adam to sleep and through the miracle of divine surgery created Eve from one of Adam's ribs. When Adam awoke, God presented Eve to him, his companion—someone to take away his loneliness problem.

In this, Almighty God is communicating that first He desires to provide for our needs—for companionship, for love, for security, for acceptance, for all our needs.

Second, He is completely and eternally capable of taking care of any of our needs we have now or ever will have in the future. He loves us all that much.

Let's go back to when God presented Eve to Adam. We can only imagine what must have gone through Adam's mind when he first saw Eve. Remember: at that first meeting she was in the buff. We're sure he was well pleased, but it's important to know that God was presenting Eve to Adam and that Adam was receiving from God a gift especially created and designed for him.

This says a lot about Adam's trust in God, because he joyfully accepted that gift, though he didn't know a thing about her. He didn't know whether she liked cereal from a box or slow-cooked oatmeal, whether she was a morning or a night person, whether she liked the room temperature cool or warm, or whether she was the type who would leave her pantyhose hanging over the shower curtain—important things like that. He simply trusted in the goodness of God.

Now here's a question for you: do you think of your mate as God's special gift to you to meet your needs? Do you trust God enough to have known what you needed and to have brought that person into your life? This even goes for you if you're now saying, "I feel as though I married the wrong person. I wasn't a Christian when I got married." God tells us in Rom. 8:28 that God is sovereign and that He can take anything, even if it's done in rebellion, and turn it into results that will achieve His purposes.

Leave and Cleave

"A man will leave his father and mother and be united [cleave] to his wife, and they will become one flesh" (Gen. 2:24).

To form the basis of a team, we need to leave, cleave, and become one. To "leave" in Hebrew means to "loosen" or "relinquish" all the ties that hold us. That could include a dependence on parents.

Yvonne: *I appreciate what my mother said to me before my wedding. She said, "I love you, but when you and Bob don't see eye to eye and you want to come home, just remember that your home is now with your husband." I was taken aback by her words at first, but as time went by I was very thankful, because I couldn't use running home as an excuse for every little negative thing. I had to work it out with Bob—together, in our home.*

Dependency could even include other family members, former spouses, or friends. No, we are to leave and cleave to our spouse. That's the meaning of Matt. 19:6, where Jesus says, "So they are no longer two, but one." The word "cleave" means "to adhere to, to stick to." It's involves the kind of adhesion you get when you use superglue. You know—the kind of glue that tends to get onto your fingers, which then get stuck to the object instead of gluing an object to an object. Yes, it's that glue that gives you a strong bond.

When you glue with superglue, you're making a commitment that you want the two objects to stick together and never to be detached again. That's the same way with marriage. You're making a commitment to your spouse to not let anything interfere with your married relationship. Anything. That means not threatening to leave or allowing your career commitment to become stronger than your marriage vows.

If you don't cleave through your commitment to your mate, you'll never have the freedom to grow and be real in your marriage, because you'll always be fearful that your spouse may leave or reject you. When we become "one flesh," it is unity through the flesh with the total person, which opens us up to be unified in *all* areas of our relationship.

This is our basis for building a team.

Team-Building Questions

1. What expectations did you bring into your marriage?
2. Where did the expectations come from? Were they realistic?
3. What has surprised you the most about marriage? Think of at least three positive aspects.
4. How would you each rate your leaving and cleaving on a scale of 1-10 (with 1 being not very good and 10 being very good)?

Discuss any area where you may be closer to the low end of the scale.

TEAM-BUILDING ACTION STEPS

In the next week separate and write down the things that attracted you to your mate. Schedule a time the two of you can be alone to go over the lists.

Father, thank You for putting us together as a team.

2

I Wish My Mate Had Come with an Instruction Manual

Team Building in Spite of Our Differences

Getting married is the main point
in life at which one says, "I have chosen;
from now on my aim will be
not to search for someone who
will please me, but to please
the one I have chosen."
—Andre Maurois

I wish God had given me an instruction manual when I married you! I just don't understand you!" Sound familiar?

There were many times both of us said that to each other. If it went unsaid, it was shouted loudly enough in our minds.

Of course, we said or thought that out of frustration when one of us couldn't understand how the other could possibly look at life that way. It didn't make any sense! All of this, of course, translated to our mate, "Why can't *you* be more like *me*? Things in our marriage would be so much better." It's like Henry Higgins singing his comedic song in *My Fair Lady*, "Why can't a woman be more like a man?"

Interesting. Before we were married we knew intellectually

24

that the way both of us looked at life was often different from the other. But it truly didn't sink in until after the wedding and we started on our journey of marriage. Not only did we more fully realize that we don't look at life the same way, but we also found in most things we didn't even think or act similarly. For instance, putting on a pair of pants.

Bob: *I go into my section of the closet and decide to try on a pair of pants I haven't put on in a couple of years. I struggle a bit and mutter, "They don't fit," so I opt for a second pair. They don't fit either. So I go to a third pair. They fit. I'm out the door.*

Yvonne: *Not me. I try on that first pair of pants, and if they don't quite fit, I don't give up. I'll lie down on the bed and struggle until I get in them. Right, ladies?*

Another example of how different we are is when we're in our car and we glance at the dashboard.

Yvonne: *Oh, oh—look at the gas gauge. It shows we're empty. You'd better pull over and get some gas now.*

Bob: *What do you mean "empty"? "E" doesn't mean "empty." "E" means "enough." Trust me—we'll make it. I'm not going to let any wimpy fumes defeat me!*

See what we mean?

Who Said What?

Or if we want to go out and eat some night.

Bob: *Honey, do you want to go out to a restaurant for dinner tonight?*

Yvonne: *Yes, that would be great.*

Bob: *OK. Where would you like to go?*

Yvonne: *Oh, I don't care. Why don't you pick it?*

Bob: *Let's see. Hmmm. How about Torotino's at Dana Point?*

Yvonne: *I don't want to go there.*

Bob: *Why not? I thought you told me to pick it!*

Yvonne: *I did, but you didn't pick the right spot.*

Anything sound familiar about *that* one? And how about when the dinner is over?

Bob: *That was delicious. Loved that swordfish. Want some dessert?*

Yvonne: *No, I'll just have a bite of yours.*

Bob: *Guys, doesn't a bite denote a single munch? Then how* *come when you drop your napkin and bend over to pick it up, it seems that she whips a mini-vacuum cleaner out of her purse and, swooossshhhh—there goes your dessert?*

Yvonne: *In defense of this alleged scenario, I don't order a dessert because I don't want a whole piece. I just want a lot of little bites of Bob's.*

Whoever said marriage was boring?

Your Backgrounds Influence How You Deal with Life

Maybe you're like us—you know that your backgrounds are not the same, but often you're not aware of how much they influence what we say and do in our marriage.

Yvonne was the oldest of three siblings. She has a brother and a sister. She shared a bedroom with her sister until she went away to college. All three of the kids shared one bathroom. In her household it wasn't unusual for all three to be brushing their teeth, spitting, and rinsing in one sink at the same time. Being simultaneously involved in the same activity was a common occurrence for them.

After we were married, when Yvonne tried to brush her teeth at the same time Bob was brushing his, he would back up a couple of steps and say to her, "You go ahead. I'll finish up after you're done." Yvonne would always try to convince Bob that it was all right to share the same space, but he wasn't convinced. He grew up as an only child and wasn't used to sharing his space. Of course, Yvonne thought there was something wrong with Bob.

Also, in reference to the previous illustration involving the dessert, Bob grew up never having to experience the fear of turning his head for a split second only to turn back and see an empty plate in front of him. Yvonne is a different story. With two young siblings on each side of her, she had to constantly protect her plate from unwanted attacks.

When it comes to sharing food, Bob is most generous. Even if he has only one bite left on his plate, if Yvonne asks for it, he shares it. Yvonne is not nearly as generous in this setting.

But the differing backgrounds don't stop there. Just being a male and female affects the way we deal with life. We fondly remember our first car trip.

Gotta Beat Last Year's Record

When we moved from Hawaii to the mainland, we relocated in the Los Angeles area. The first long car trip we took was to be for nearly 800 miles. Now on the island of Oahu one doesn't take long car trips. It seems that by the time you shift into fourth gear, no matter what direction you're headed, you'll wind up in the water. This was going to be a new experience for us. Yvonne is the social director of the family, so she was planning a fabulous trip.

Yvonne: *I planned that we'd leave early before the 22 million cars descended into the Los Angeles area. We'd drive a couple of hours and then stop for a leisurely breakfast. Drive for a few more hours, then do some sight-seeing and shopping. Drive two more hours, then stop for lunch and more shopping. I thought that was a wonderful plan, but do you think that was Bob's idea of a trip?*

Bob: *Guys, isn't the main idea of the day to get to where you're going as fast as you can and to try to beat last year's record by at least 20 minutes?*

Yvonne: *No, the idea is to enjoy the process. Enjoy the scenery. Enjoy the trip.*

Bob: *The process is meaningless. It's the results that count. I enjoy it if I conquer it. And I dislike having to pull into those rest stops all the time. I'm known as Camel Bladder Bob. I can, if you know what I mean, "hold it" from motel to motel. I don't need a rest stop. Granted, when I get to the motel in the evening I may have tears in my eyes, and I practically knock the door down getting into my room, but, hey—I made it. But not Yvonne. We have to pull into what seems like every other rest stop. And while I'm tapping my toes waiting impatiently, I can see all those trucks I passed on the interstate zipping down the freeway honking their horns, and I'm sure they're waving and laughing at me.*

Is There Really a Difference in Our Brains?

As you can see, males and females are very different. Even the way we watch television.

Yvonne: *Wives, have you ever tried to get your husband's attention while he's focused on a TV program? Can you do it? It has to do with the differences in a man's brain and a woman's brain.*

In recent years scientists have studied the human brain and

found that even though both the male and female brains are made up of two halves, a right and left hemisphere, the way they function is quite different.

A man's brain functions more like a compartment. If he's watching TV, his brain is open in the TV compartment, and that's where he's mainly focused. If he wants to have a conversation with his spouse, he closes the TV compartment and opens the conversation compartment. He's then focused there. Because his brain was designed to be more single-minded, he is not so easily distracted and can shut out everything that can distract him. He gets very focused, like a laser beam.

That's why you have a hard time getting his attention when he watches TV or reads the newspaper. In fact, have you ever noticed that he could be in the family room watching *Victory at Sea* on the History Channel, totally unaware that a few feet from him the kids are having an all-out sibling brawl? A woman often has a hard time realizing that although his physical body is there, he's not really there. It's difficult, because her brain works differently.

At our marriage conferences we often ask the men, "Have you ever watched your wife watch TV? Then you've noticed that many times she may not even be in the same room as the television set. If she *is* in the same room, then at the same time she can also write checks for the bills, talk on the phone to her sister, rub the puppy's back with her foot, know where the kids are in the house, and be aware of what the neighbors on each side are doing."

The reason for this is that her brain operates more holistically. The bundle of nerve fibers that link the right side of the brain to the left side are used for the exchange of information between the two halves. In a woman's brain the bundle is bigger, so she has more connectors than a man. For her more information is exchanged.

She uses different parts on both sides of her brain at one time. Her brain isn't a laser beam but rather is more like a radar that is constantly scanning, which allows her to tune into everything around her. This makes her more perceptive of people and their feelings. This accounts for her knowing that a couple across the room, even though smiling, are having trouble in their relationship.

Opposites Attract—Then They Attack

We have found that when opposites attract, they attack. One spouse feels the other is wrong in his or her approach to life and would be so much better off by changing a behavior. In Joe Tanenbaum's book *Male and Female Realities,* the author demonstrates this difference. He conducted workshops and over a period of time had his participants write out what they would change if they could "fix" the opposite sex. Here are the results:

WOMEN WOULD	MEN WOULD
Talk less	Talk more
Be less emotional	Be more emotional
Be less "romantic"	Be more "romantic"
Want more sex	Want less sex
Be more rational	Be more spontaneous
Laugh less	Lighten up; be silly
Put job/career first	Put family first
Spend less time getting ready	Give more attention on hygiene
Be on time	Be more flexible with time[1]

Did you notice that every one of the items on the women's list is exactly the opposite of those on the men's? Have *you* ever had similar thoughts? We both have.

Yvonne remembers one time being so frustrated about our differences that she cried out to the Lord, "Why didn't You make us more similar? That way my life would be so much easier!" She felt these frustrations would cease if we were just more alike. At the pinnacle of her frustration God started to reveal to her why He had put together two very different people and that she was to trust Him because He had a plan that was the best for our marriage. He has a plan that is best for your marriage too. God's ultimate goal for every Christian is that we become more like His Son, Jesus. Marriage is a tool that God uses to help us in our growth as believers. As we learn more about who we are, it helps us discover our strengths as well as our weaknesses. This concept can be compared to a rock-polishing kit.

Did You Ever Use a Rock-Polishing Kit?

Both of us used rock-polishing kits when we were in elementary school. We took rough-hewn rocks and placed them in the rock-polishing cylinder and added sand, which serves as grit. When we turned the machine on, the rocks would roll over and over onto each other with the grit in between them, which slowly smoothed the stones over a long period of time. When we turned off the machine and pulled out the stones, they were smooth—no longer rough.

That typifies marriage. In a manner of speaking, we can look upon our spouse as grit, or "heavenly sandpaper." It's because of our differences that we rub up against each other and at times bother each other. But through this process we are being polished into the likeness of Christ. Prov. 27:17 says, "As iron sharpens iron, so one man sharpens another." A marriage view of that verse would read, "As iron sharpens iron, so one spouse sharpens the other."

He Placed Us Together for Completion, Not Competition

It is through this process that a marriage team is being built. God placed us together for completion, not competition. In Gen. 2:18 God speaks about being a complement as He says, "It is not good for the man to be alone. I will make a helper suitable for him." In the Hebrew, "helper" means *complement*. To us that means God is giving a mate a *gift*, who will complete us. God knew who you needed. He certainly knew who *we* needed.

Look at a football team—any level, whether peewee or pro. During practice the players are in competition with each other to be named to the first string. But after the starting unit is formed and an actual game begins, the players should no longer be in competition with each other, but against the opposing team. If they don't play as a unified team and each member is trying to be a superstar, then the whole becomes weak. Each team member must know he is valuable and has something to offer to the team, recognizing that he and his teammates are no longer in competition with each other but are to complement each other, functioning as one unit against their competitor. This is what Eccles. 4:9-12 speaks about: "Two are better than one, because they have a good return for their work: If one falls down, his friend can help him up. But pity the man who falls and has no one to help him up! Also, if two lie down together, they will keep warm. But how can one keep warm alone? Though one may be overpowered, two can defend themselves. A cord of three strands is not quickly broken."

Thankfully, we have found that in our marriage that third strand is God. We need Him, and we need each other.

In our marriage relationship we need each other in a variety of ways. Take for example some of the times we were in our car headed for a particular destination. Yvonne would mention to Bob, "Don't forget—we're supposed to take the next exit."

Bob would get a bit huffy with that reminder and say, "I know. I know." Translation: "I remember. I'll handle the driving—thank you. I really don't need your help."

Yvonne: *The only reason I would mention it is because I know that even though Bob's body may be in the car, his highly creative mind often wanders so far into outer space that even the Hubble telescope couldn't locate it. That's why we've often zipped past our exits. I just want to help. In this case we were working against each other and not as a team.*

One day after driving home alone, Bob said to Yvonne, "Honey, you can refresh my memory any time you want on what exits I'm to take, because earlier today I was 'floating' and zipped past my exit. I had to go a couple of miles to the next one and then double back. What a waste of time! I must confess—I need you as my copilot."

Now in the car we're a *team*. We work together on getting to our destination.

We also believe that God created us to complete each other. Have you ever wondered why God didn't make just *one* person, Adam, totally complete in himself, not needing anyone? We believe it was to teach him he was not self-sufficient—that he had needs that he could not take care of himself. We're like Adam as we realize that we need someone else—our mate—to complement us. That points us to God. Even through the uniqueness of God creating a male-female relationship, we still can't do it all by ourselves. No, we need God.

The Two A's of Marriage Team Building

As mentioned previously, opposites attract—then they attack. They attack each other because of their differences. But

God's plan for a marriage is for us to learn and accept and appreciate those differences. We call these our *"A's of marriage team building."*

Let's look at *acceptance* first. Accept your mate for who he or she is rather than for your own personal remodeling project. One of the strongest needs we all have is for acceptance. None of us likes to be rejected. As kids we didn't want to be the last one picked when the captains were choosing teams. We do many things in order to prevent the sting of rejection.

In marriage the need for acceptance is very strong, but too often we show more rejection than acceptance. We let our mate know in a couple of ways that he or she didn't measure up to what we expected. We may show it when he or she says or does something we didn't like, so we give him or her "that look." A spouse will usually respond with "What? What did I do [or say] now?"

Or we may demonstrate our rejection with an *attitude.* You ask, "What's wrong?" The response you get is a sigh, eyes looking down, and a quiet monotone voice that says, "Oh—nothing."

"No, no. Tell me. What's wrong? I must have done or said something. *Tell* me."

Or we show it with words something like this: "Good grief! I can't believe you just did that!"

Rejection does not build unity or team spirit. Instead of drawing your mate closer to you, it just pushes him or her away. That's what we were doing to each other in the early years of our marriage. From the first day of our marriage, Yvonne started to develop her remodeling job and created a "fix it" list on Bob. Nothing was written down, but it was a mental list Yvonne was storing away in her brain. The list grew by leaps and bounds year after year. When Bob would do or say something she disliked, she was famous for giving him "that look" and would immediately add it to her "fix it" list, all the time thinking, "If Bob would just make some obviously needed changes, he would be much better off and we'd have a better marriage." After several years of this, he started giving Yvonne what we call "R and R."

"R and R" is best remembered from the time of the Vietnam War as "rest and recuperation" (or recreation). But what Bob was giving Yvonne was the in-your-face, in-the-trenches-of-your-home R and R: "resist and retreat." When someone gets hammered often enough and long enough, he or she will resist but after a while can say, "Oh, bag it. This is a joke. I'll stay married, but emotionally I'm outta here." So they retreat. That's what Bob did.

God does not desire that kind of R and R in any of the marriages of His children. In Rom. 15:7 Paul writes, "Accept one another, then, just as Christ accepted you, in order to bring praise to God."

Since this verse was written to the Body of Christ, and if a husband and wife are both Christians, then we look at this verse as just as much a marriage verse as a general verse to all believers. To rephrase it we could say, "Husbands and wives, accept your spouse, then, just as Christ accepted you, and when you do that you will bring praise to God." We are to accept our mate as Christ accepts us—with complete, unconditional love. Think of God's acceptance of you. Did He ever say, "When you, [fill in your name], get your act together and clean up all your hang-ups, then *maybe* I'll accept you—but until that time, no way." We're thankful that Rom. 5:8 says, "But God demonstrates his own love for us in this: While we were still sinners, Christ died for us."

God loved and accepted each of us right where we were when we entered into a love relationship with Him. It has been through that acceptance that we started to grow and change. It can be the same with our mate. Look at the rest of Rom. 15:7, where it says that by doing this you will "bring praise to God." That's right—simply by accepting your spouse as Christ accepts you, God is praised.

No, You Don't Accept Affairs

After we had spoken at a marriage retreat, a woman came to us afterward and said, "After hearing your message, I guess I'm supposed to accept the fact that my husband has had a number of affairs."

We told her that is *not* what acceptance means. No, you don't accept immoral behavior. We're not to accept sin.

In our marriage we don't accept all the behavior our mate

does because, frankly, some behavior needs to be addressed and changed, such as with this woman's husband. We shouldn't ignore situations. Otherwise we become an enabler, which means we enable them to keep doing their destructive behavior. Instead, we should be honest about our mate's faults without condemning. Instead, extend grace. We need to follow the biblical injunction found in Gal. 6:1: "Brothers and sisters, if someone in your group does something wrong, you who are spiritual should go to that person and gently help make him right again. But be careful, because you might be tempted to sin, too" (NCV). Yes, you might deal with a behavior that may require some tough love. You also need to set up boundaries, but do it through good communication.

Don't Be a Speck Inspector

How do you go about accepting your mate if *you* haven't been accepted? Good question. Yvonne asked that same question and received an answer in Jesus' words of Matt. 7:3-5: "Why do you look at the speck of sawdust in your brother's eye and pay no attention to the plank in your own eye? How can you say to your brother, 'Let me take the speck out of your eye,' when all the time there is a plank in your own eye? You hypocrite, first take the plank out of your own eye, and then you will see clearly to remove the speck from your brother's eye."

Yvonne discovered she had become a "speck inspector." She was terrific at seeing and pointing out all the specks in Bob's eyes but couldn't see the plank sticking out of her own eye. What a funny verbal visual! Can't you just picture Yvonne walking around bumping Bob with her own monstrous plank but never even noticing it?

We'll always have a hard time changing our mate, but we *can* change ourselves. That's where God wanted to begin with Yvonne.

Yvonne was learning that by not accepting Bob and by showing rejection of him, she was in essence rejecting what God was saying was best for her. Remember—your mate is God's gift to you, to complete you.

Yvonne: *Here I was not trusting God enough to know what was best for me and telling Him I knew better than He did what I needed. So to stop me from being a speck inspector, I needed to view Bob* *through God's eyes. I needed to put on my "Jesus glasses" each morning. As I put them on I would pray that I would look at Bob the way God sees him, through the eyes of Jesus. Big difference. I discovered that certain things that used to bug me about Bob just didn't bother me anymore. I also started to view our differences not as weaknesses or irritations, but simply as differences. The Lord helped me learn to accept and not always reject. At the same time I started to believe and understand that God had indeed placed the two of us together. We complemented each other.*

I was also assuming that Bob's differences were wrong and that my way was right. Oh, not all the time, but certainly most of the time. That attitude showed immaturity. I had to realize that my way was simply one way of looking at a situation, and his way was another way.

I was so busy trying to make Bob into my image. My thoughts were that everything would be better if Bob would just—you've heard it before, or maybe you've said it: "If he would have done it the way I told him, it would have turned out better." But in Eph. 5:1 we are told, "Be imitators of God, therefore, as dearly loved children."

Our Hands and Marriage Should Intermingle

Take your left hand now and place it in front of you. Spread your fingers out. Take your right hand and do the same with it. Now that they're both in front of you, place both hands together with fingers intermingled. They fit together, don't they? Each hand fills in the gaps of the other hand.

That's exactly how it is with a married couple and the way God desires for us to view it.

Take our personality differences. Yvonne is a planner. When she goes somewhere she wants to know where she's going, how she's getting there, and how long it will take. Bob's personality is what you would call a "winger." Why plan so much? Life is an adventure. Let's just see what happens along the way. Can you tell we have two different perspectives on life?

Bob used to say to Yvonne, "Lighten up. You need to enjoy life more."

Yvonne would say to Bob, "Things would be so much better in your life if you'd just get more organized."

Yvonne: *Even though I didn't see it at first, God knew that I needed Bob to balance me. With my overplanning I was becoming so* *inflexible I felt that I was breaking in two. Guess who God sent to me? That's right — a winger.*

Bob: *God knew I needed to get a little more organized, so guess who He put into my life? You got it. The planning queen herself, Yvonne, who, by the way, has greatly helped me do just that — get a plan.*

The kicker to all this is that we balance each other out when we work together as a team in our speaking ministry. When we put together a seminar, conference, or retreat, we now have planning with flexibility, along with fun, while making sure there's a point to it all.

The first *A* of team building is to accept your mate. Period. The second *A* of team building is to appreciate your mate for what he or she has done.

"I've heard so much about you from your wife," Yvonne said to a man who was introduced to her.

His quick retort was "She probably told you all the things that are wrong with me."

Yvonne: *I had known his wife for quite some time and knew that she and her husband were having some major struggles in their relationship, but I was also aware that anytime she spoke about him she would only say nice things, so I responded with "No, quite the contrary. She told me what a great father you are to the kids and how hard you work to provide for the family."*

He was quite taken aback by that, looked surprised, and replied, "Who said that?"

"Your wife."

He stared with a blank look for a moment or two, and then we went our own ways. This conversation was a turning point in their relationship. Because of their struggles, the wife wanted the two of them to meet with us, but the husband was never open to that. Mainly he thought it would be a waste of time, because he also thought she never really cared about him since she allegedly never said anything positive. In his ears all he ever heard was what was wrong with him, never about anything being right. So he was thinking, "Why see someone when there's no hope for my marriage?"

But based on what Yvonne told him, he then thought, "Hmmm—maybe she does care more about me than I realized." He agreed to see both of us and to work on improving their marriage.

We All Hunger to Be Appreciated

Surveys have shown for years that in the workplace people will work harder for praise than they will for a raise. Yes, we all like raises, but what's more important to the majority is to know that what they do or who they are matters to someone.

Many think, "Why work so hard if the only time the boss wants to see me is to chew me out?" That's not motivating. That is *de*-motivating.

The same holds true in our families. If your mate has done something nice for you, maybe even a special favor, but you don't say thank you in some way or even recognize the favor, it certainly won't be long until the niceness stops. Your spouse thinks, "Hey, if he/she doesn't even notice it, why bother?" It de-motivates them.

Nag-Sag Vs. Praise-Raise

We heard a wonderful phrase many years ago: "If you nag, their shoulders sag, but if you praise, their shoulders raise" [sic]. Can't you just picture that? Whether spouse to spouse, parent to child, coach to athlete, teacher to student, employer to employee, or whatever the situation—if you nag at people continuously, their shoulders sag, but if you praise them continuously, their shoulders rise. Another way of saying that is "Their *spirits* rise."

One of the main reasons we fell into the nag-sag category was we weren't giving praise to each other. Instead, we were getting focused on what we thought was *wrong* with our spouse rather than on what was *right*. Our home became more of a "dumping station" than a "filling station." At a "filling station" you get filled up with all the good stuff that prepares you to go out to battle the world, whether at work or school. We don't need to comment further on the "dumping station." Too many people have sadly experienced that too often.

Why Do We Always Learn Lessons the Hard Way?

We learned a lesson the hard way in our family once when the two of us went away for a weekend retreat. It was a family conference, and we were the speakers. Robert, our son, was 16 at the time, and he was going to be home alone under the watchful care of a neighbor while we were away. We left him with four jobs to accomplish prior to our return.

We "perfect" parents returned home on a Sunday afternoon from teaching other parents how to be perfect like us, and as we drove into our garage we glanced over to one of the corners and noted that one of the jobs we gave Robert to do wasn't done.

Yvonne: *I remember saying caustically, "That figures."*

Bob: *And I remember saying, "Well, I'm sure going to have a talk with him."*

So Bob barged into the house, and there young Robert was vegging out on the couch in the family room watching television. He got up, smiled, and with his hand giving a welcome-home wave, opened his mouth to speak, but Bob bellowed first, "Robert, how come you didn't do that garage task we asked you to do before we left?"

With Junior's smile fading and his hand limp in the air, he quietly said, "Welcome home, Dad. How did the retreat go? I was praying for you all weekend."

Whoops! Strike one. A moment of awkward silence from both of us as Yvonne had walked in and heard the two-way chat.

Bob: *I remembered muttering some kind of weak excuse under my breath, but before another beat went by, Robert said, "Dad, didn't you notice the three jobs that I did do?" Whoops! Strike two.*

Yvonne: *Do you think we did notice them? Nope, as with so many other spouses or parents, we seemed to notice what wasn't done before we noticed what was done, or we saw what was wrong before we saw what was right.*

Bob: *But you, reader, are probably the same way. Whenever you have a flat tire, do you thank the other three tires for staying intact? No way! We're all so busy mumbling over the flat one that we don't see the other three tires flexing their treads, shouting at us, "Hey — we're loyal! How about us?" Nope, we concentrate on what's wrong.*

Young Turnbull then said, "Dad, the reason I didn't do the garage job is that the tool I needed to do it with was in the trunk of your car all weekend." Whoops! Strike three.

All we could do was laugh. We apologized to Robert profusely, asked his forgiveness, and then vowed that from then on we would notice what was right in our family before we noticed what was wrong. That's right—we three agreed there was going to be a family change. From now on our home would be deemed a "filling station."

Shortly after we agreed upon that change, Yvonne attended a women's conference. One of the speakers suggested to the married women that when they returned home they write down 10 praiseworthy things about their mate. Then each day for 10 days they were to give their husband one of the praises.

Yvonne: *When I heard that, I said, "That's easy. I'm getting into this praise thing. I can do that."*

So Yvonne excitedly went home, and as soon as she could, she sat down with a blank piece of paper to whip off those 10 praiseworthy sentences.

Yvonne: *I was feeling smug, so I quickly wrote down that first one. Piece of cake. Then I jotted down the second one. It took me a bit to think of that third one, and when it came time to write number four, I was stuck. I couldn't get past three. I wasn't stuck because Bob didn't have many great qualities, but this assignment made me aware that I had spent far too much time in our relationship focusing on the negative.*

Maybe you're currently like what Yvonne was. Maybe right now your thoughts are in the arena of "There aren't too many good things about my mate to focus on." If that's the case and you're ready for a change, here's a way to do it. We call this method "think-thank-tell."

Step One—Think

Think. Yvonne realized that she needed to change her focus and center it on all the things she was grateful for regarding Bob. So she started praying.

Yvonne: *"Lord, please open my eyes to the areas that are right about my husband. I know there are many, but I've been blinded to them with my wrong thinking."* God did just that, and I began to see my husband differently and started to notice many things about him that I had often overlooked or taken for granted.

Part of that renewed thinking involves looking at what you have focused on and then changing it. A Bible verse that helped change not just Yvonne's focus but Bob's too is Phil. 4:8: "Whatever is true, whatever is noble, whatever is right, whatever is pure, whatever is lovely, whatever is admirable—if anything is excellent or praiseworthy—*think about such things*" (emphasis added). We both think on those things—regularly.

What Yvonne did first to change her focus was to complete that list of 10 things about Bob for which she was grateful to God. She then put it where she could read it aloud daily. This method works well with parents of children, especially at those times when the parents are upset with the wee ones. Even though hassles and hurts need to be fairly dealt with, this method still helps a parent keep the focus on what the child does *right*.

Step Two—Thank

Thank. 2 Cor. 9:15 says, "Thanks be to God for his indescribable gift!" That gift is His grace. This verse encouraged us to thank Him for the mate He put into our lives and for His help to see him or her differently.

Thanking God changes our focus. It's like Yvonne when she's out in the garden tending her rosebushes. There was one day in particular when she was pruning one of the bushes that had overgrown. She found herself grumbling about the thorns each time one pricked her.

Yvonne: *After about 15 minutes of grumbling, a thought came to my mind. I had a choice. I could continue to grumble because the roses have thorns, or I could change my focus and thank God that on a thornbush He created such beautiful roses for my enjoyment.*

It's all in the focus. Same circumstances, but different focus.

Right now thank the Lord for your mate. Yes, right now. It's amazing how an attitude of thankfulness changes the way you look at the circumstances. We are blessed to let God know *every* day what we're thankful for.

Step Three—Tell

Tell. Prov. 3:27 reads, "Do not withhold good from those who deserve it, when it is in your power to act." And it's *always* in our power to act when the Holy Spirit has His freedom within us. Let your mate know what you've noticed.

The word "praise" comes from a Latin word for "worth." When we give praise to our mate, we're telling our mate we think he or she is worthwhile.

Four tips that can help you in giving praise to your spouse:

1. Be specific about those things he or she does. "I appreciate the way you always anticipate my need for clean socks in my drawer." "I like the way you will listen to me when I feel as if I'm coming unglued." "Thanks for taking out the trash every night." "Wow! You look great—a first-class knockout."

2. Be sincere. Know the difference between praise and flattery. Flattery is making something sound better than it actually is. It is insincere and is often used to manipulate another to get what you want. Prov. 26:28 says, "Flattery is a form of hatred and wounds cruelly" (TLB). But when we're honest in our praise, we attribute value to the other person and encourage him or her to keep going.

3. Be generous. Do it frequently. Trust us—we would be surprised if your mate said to you, "Please stop praising me. I've had too much."

4. Be creative. Since you're giving it frequently, you can change the way praise is delivered, from verbal to written. We often leave small notes around the house with words of praise to each other.

God has used the "think-thank-tell" method to change both of us, which in turn has deeply impacted our marriage.

Team-Building Questions

1. Ask your mate if he or she thinks you show acceptance to him or her. If your mate feels you don't, ask how you demonstrate it. List two or three ways.
2. Ask your mate what he or she would like you to do specifically to show acceptance.
3. Together write a list of the strengths of each of you. Examine the list to see how you complement each other. Develop a plan to put these strengths together so you can be a better marriage team.

Team-Building Action Steps

1. If either of you are "speck inspectors" and need a log removal oper-

ation, the following is a process to follow. Each spouse does this alone.

Take a piece of paper and draw a vertical line down the middle. On the lefthand side, list the differences in your mate's life that trigger a negative response from you. For example, "My mate always leaves things that need to be done until the very last minute." On the right side list your own inappropriate responses (such as nagging, getting angry, and so on). Admit to God (1 John 1:9) your wrong response. Throw the list away and then apologize to your mate. Now talk to your mate about how you can work this situation out. You may have an area of strength that could help.

2. For the next 12 days give your mate a daily dose of praise by administering a "one-a-day praise vitamin." It can be given morning, afternoon, or night. To help you, read Phil. 4:8, and with each word in the verse make a list of things you can praise your mate for.

Father, help us view ourselves —
and our weaknesses — with a magnifying glass,
and help us see our mate through a telescope.

Building Block No. 2
Roles and Expectations

3

How to Be a Champion of a Husband

Team Building Through the Husband's Role

He who does not honor his wife dishonors himself.
—Spanish proverb

*I*f you've been a husband for any length of time, by now you have to know that your wife is very different from you. The main reason is that she's a female and you're a male. Yes, we could say, "Case closed," but allow us to add a few more ingredients to the mix.

One mix is that since we're so different, as male and female, we are affected by what we each think is funny. Picture a group of men and women in a room, watching television, and an episode of "The Three Stooges" comes on. The men will yell out, "All right!" and then laugh loudly at the antics of these three buffoons, especially of their favorite stooge, Curly. The women will mumble "This is ridiculous!" sigh, hope this isn't a Stooges marathon weekend, and be impatient until the show is finally over.

The differences also affect the way we would each furnish a bathroom. A husband has some basic items in his bathroom: a toothbrush, toothpaste, shaving cream, razor, hairbrush, a bar of soap, and a towel. The average number of items in a wife's bathroom is 386, and her husband would be able to identify only about 12 of these items.

Our clothing serves different purposes, like the wearing of

socks. A husband will wear what he considers sensible socks—standard white sweatsocks. He thinks his wife wears really weird socks—socks that are cut way below the ankles, socks that have pictures of rainbows, socks that have a fuzzy ball on the back.

Even the telephone has a different use, depending on whether you're male or female. A husband sees it as an important tool for communication. He will use it to send crisp, short messages to other people. His wife, however, can go out of town to spend a week with her best friend and then return home only to rush to the telephone, call that same friend, and talk for two hours.

Guys, have you noticed that your wife will sometimes admit to making a mistake? The last man who admitted he was wrong was Japanese Emperor Hirohito in 1945. And what about the way we look at time? When your wife says she'll be ready to go out in just five more minutes, she's using the same meaning of time you do when you say, "What's that, Hon? Oh, the football game will be over in just five minutes." Neither of them is including commercials, time-outs, and replays.

And, of course, let's not forget the different way we use rest rooms when we are out for a social event. Men use the rest room for a bodily function. Women use the rest room as a social lounge. Men in rest rooms don't talk to each other. Women who have never met will leave a rest room laughing together like old friends. And never, repeat, *never* in the history of humanity has a man excused himself from a restaurant table by saying, "Hey, Ted—I'm going to the rest room. Care to join me?"

Men and women look at life and deal with it so very differently!

One main difference is that God created women with an emotional need for security. Everything she does and everything she says is rooted in that basic need. That's why she'll sometimes ask you, "Do you love me?" She needs the reassurance of your love because it makes her feel secure in her marriage to you.

Or perhaps she awakes in the middle of the night to a sound she thinks she hears somewhere in the house. You, of course, are snoring away and hear nothing. She wakes you up and has you check the house to make sure everything is all right. She says she'll stay in bed and pray for you as you stumble throughout the dark house, banging your knees on various pieces of furniture. Security.

The good news is God created the husband with the capacity to meet his wife's need for security, and He did so by the way he wired men. And since God created that wiring, He has also given men instructions in His Holy Word as to how to meet that need through the role of a husband. The same is true with a woman. She's able to meet her husband's need for significance because of the role God has given her to fulfill. When a husband and wife fulfill their different roles, it assists the marriage to function as a team instead of a fragmented mess.

It's like a male-female ice-skating team. Two people—a man and a woman—come together in form and balance, with each partner separate, each movement unique yet somehow complementary and essential to the other. That's the way the husband and wife roles work in a marriage.

The basis for the role a husband is to fulfill in marriage is found in Eph. 5:23, 25-30 "The husband is the head of the wife as Christ is the head of the church, his body, of which he is the Savior. . . . Husbands, love your wives, just as Christ loved the church and gave himself up for her to make her holy, cleansing her by the washing with water through the word, and to present her to himself as a radiant church, without stain or wrinkle or any other blemish, but holy and blameless. In this same way, husbands ought to love their wives as their own bodies. He who loves his wife loves himself. After all, no one ever hated his own body, but he feeds and cares for it, just as Christ does the church—for we are members of his body."

The scriptures instruct the husband to meet his wife's need for security by loving her and leading her. In this chapter we're going to look at *leading* her.

Lead Your Wife

When Paul wrote to the Ephesians about a husband's responsibility within the marriage, those words were considered radical. The culture then was so different that he most likely offended many in that time period, because the Roman Empire was flourishing militarily and financially, most of the citizens lived in urban areas, transportation was fluid to all parts of the empire, and life was good. Ironically, even in the midst of all this affluence, the family was stressed and near the breaking point. The divorce rate was skyrocketing. Women were bored with domestic life and sought fulfillment outside of the home. Motherhood was devalued more and more, so many women were deciding it wasn't worth it to bear children, and thus the birthrate declined.

More and more couples were seeking their own selfish, independent lifestyle. Husbands didn't want to bother being the leader in the family, and the wives didn't want to be led. Does this sound anything like modern-day society?

So it was in this downwardly spiraling culture that Paul wrote what he did. He wasn't pronouncing what the current pop trend was or trying to encourage them to return to something they had lost. No, what he was speaking and writing was new, different, and highly controversial. As we look at God's way instead of humanity's way we'll discover that His way is not binding and unsatisfying, but instead is freeing and fulfilling.

In Eph. 5:23 Paul says the husband is the head of the wife. People often ask, "What does 'head' mean?" Another word for "head" is "leader." That's why we say that God has given the husband the *responsibility* of leading his wife. But keep in mind that a husband was not placed in this role because God created him in any way to be superior to his wife. If that were the case, then one would have to also say that God is superior to Jesus Christ, but we know that Jesus is equal to God yet is subject to Him (1 Cor. 11:3).

The roles given to a husband and wife are positions of responsibility, not rank. Simply put, a husband and wife are not superior or inferior to each other. Yes, they are different roles, but they are of equal value.

In Gal. 3:28 Paul writes, "In Christ, there is no difference between Jew and Greek, slave and free person, male and female. You are *all the same* in Christ Jesus" (NCV, emphasis added).

We think the reason so many people interpret the words "head" and "leader" as being superior is that they believe Paul, the writer of the Ephesians verses, was describing a military hierarchial ranking system, in which one position is higher than another. He wasn't. He was using it as a physical metaphor.

Tim Kimmel in his book *Basic Training for a Few Good Men* says that the two different positions in the marriage are like the relationship between the heart and the lungs. Kimmel asks, "If you had to pick one of the two organs to do without, which one would you pick? Obviously you can't part with either one of them, plus the heart and the lungs work as a team. One cleans the blood while the other pumps it through the rest of the system. Your wife is to be viewed not as inferior or subordinate, but as an equal who serves a different function in the relationship from the one you have."[1]

Being the Leader Doesn't Mean Being "The Boss"

A 33-year-old man named Joe attended one of our marriage seminars. During one of our breaks he said to us, "I heard what you said about my role in the family is to be the leader, so I was wondering how to get my wife to do what I want her to do."

Bob: *I knew I had my job cut out for me during the next session of the seminar, but I also realized this guy needed something to think about even before the next session started. I thought for a moment and then said to him, "Leadership in marriage is not about getting. It's about giving."*

Oswald Chambers said, "True greatness, true leadership, is achieved not by reducing men to one's service, but by giving up oneself in selfless service to them." This is the leadership a husband is to give to his wife and family. He is a servant, not a ruler.

Servant Leadership

A husband is to model Jesus' style of leadership to his family. This is outlined in Mark 10:42-43, 45, in which He said, "The [other nations] have rulers. You know that those rulers love to show their power over people, and their important leaders love to use all their authority. But it should not be that way among you. Whoever wants to become great among you must serve the rest of you like a servant. . . . the Son of Man did not come to be served. He came to serve others" (NCV).

Bob: *To me this means a husband should try to "outserve" his wife.*

Reread the first part of those verses. Can't you see that as fitting some of our rulers today? Unfortunately, many husbands are doing the same thing. They're looking for the hottest chief executive officers, political wizards, or super sports stars as their role models. They end up using force and power to enrich themselves. They want to receive all the perks and benefits they believe are due them, but it usually happens at the expense of others, and in a family that means the wife and kids.

Phillip comes home from work, plops himself down in front of the TV set, grabs his newspaper, and waits for his wife, Becky, to get home from work after picking up their kids at the day care center. It would never dawn on him to start the dinner or even help the kids with their homework when they get home. He rationalizes that he has worked hard all day and that it's now time for the king to sit on his throne and relax. Plus, he thinks, "That stuff is woman's work."

At the same time Becky is very tired from her hard day's work, yet she spends the night busily trying to take care of everybody's needs. She's on the run from the moment she wakes up and hits the floor until she drops exhausted into bed late at night. Phillip is concerned only about his own needs and what Becky can give him in this relationship. His leadership of the family is based on his own self-interests and the *love of power*, rather than being based on servant leadership and the *power of love.*

Look at how these two differ:

Love of Power	vs.	Power of Love
Focuses on own needs		Focuses on the needs of others
Demands		Discusses
Desires to get		Desires to give
Is selfish		Is a servant
Is self-motivated		Is Holy Spirit-enabled

When a man is leading by the love of power, he often falls into either one of two extremes of leadership. Neither is effective. One is the dictator husband; the other is the passive husband.

The Dictator Husband

Bob: *We both recall a session that followed a sermon we gave at a church service. While talking to a group of people, we became uncom-*

fortably aware that one woman would never speak unless she first glanced at her husband to see if he nodded his head her direction, thus granting her permission to speak. This happened each time we talked with them.

This man obviously positions himself as "the boss." He gives all the orders and makes all the decisions. His favorite motto is probably "You will do it *my* way." That's not leadership—that's dictatorship.

Yvonne: *A woman came up to us during another one of our seminars and said that so often when she would bring something up, her husband would say, "You don't know what you're talking about." She said this would effectively silence her, because she knew that no matter what she would say next, he was going to do everything he could in order to win.*

Dictator husbands tend to become defensive if a family member states an opinion or idea that is contrary to his own. That becomes a threat to him, especially if he has the mind-set that he is supposed to be in control of everybody and everything. So in order to preserve himself and his possible feelings of inferiority, he will exert more control over his wife and children by manipulating them until he assures himself that he has come out the winner.

After reading about the dictator, you may be saying, "Hey—that's not me. I'm not harsh like that guy." Well, read on, for you just might qualify for the other extreme. This leader is called "the passive husband."

The Passive Husband

Bob: *We know a classic example of this one—we once had a neighbor who was a 100 percent passive husband. Whenever his wife would bring up a problem in the family that needed attention, he invariably ignored her and would ride out the wave. If she brought it up again, he would call her a nag. Procrastination and indecision were his trademarks.*

Over a period of time we noticed our neighbor controlling his family by sitting back and watching his marriage and family instead of being an active participant. Just about anytime his wife or kids asked him about something, his reply was "Whatever." We could see he didn't want to be held accountable for anything, and he basically got his wish of not having to bother with the hassles of a family life. By doing this, he clearly demonstrated that he was concerned only about himself and did not desire to give the family what they needed—his leadership.

The passive role of leadership is not necessarily because of the man's personality. As one wife told us at one of our summer family camps, "My husband is a dynamo at work. He's busy planning, organizing, and doing, but when he comes home it's as if he puts his blinders and ear plugs on, and he neither sees nor hears the needs of his family."

The passive husband may have started out with the best intentions of being *head,* but something happened along the way. We've found that that "something" usually falls into four categories that cause him to cast himself in the passive role.

1. Wife's Resistance

In some cases, a husband may have tried to be the *head* or *leader,* but he's come across so much resistance from his wife that he finally throws in the towel and starts living out the attitude of "Why bother?"

2. Not Seeing a Need

His wife is fairly independent, so he doesn't really see a need to be a head or leader. She may have a capable personality, but to function properly and feel secure in the marriage, she needs his leadership.

3. Fear of Failure

He overinvests in activities, especially his job, so he has no time to lead. Often his busyness can be from a fear that his wife won't follow him if he did try to lead. Satan wants to snag you in his quicksand of fear. He wants you to believe that you'll never be successful, so why try? Remember: Satan is the author of lies (John 8:44), but we need to depend on the Author of truth. God says He will equip you with everything you need to succeed as a godly leader (Phil. 4:13).

4. No Role Model

When he grew up he didn't have a father or any other man who modeled the role of a husband, so he may perceive his role incorrectly, which causes him not to lead in a biblical way.

That's where the role of a mentor could be of tremendous benefit. Every husband should pray and look for an older godly man that God will bring into his life.

Gut-and-Soul Check

Right now ask yourself some questions:
- When dealing with my family, am I more concerned about what I want or what would be best for everyone involved?
- Do I make selfish demands, such as, "Listen—*I'm* the husband [father] and the head of this house, so you'll do what *I* say—there'll be no discussion about this"? Or am I open to what others in the family think and the alternatives they may present?
- Do I just "let life happen" so the family is chasing after everything that comes along that looks inviting and tempting, or do I have a vision for my family and thus set the direction for them so everybody is working together to accomplish that vision? God is going to hold you responsible for the direction and condition of your family.

Bob: *For years in our marriage I hadn't been functioning as a servant leader. I wanted Yvonne to serve me. Because of that, our marriage wasn't growing. In fact, it was going from bad to worse because of my attitude.*

But I experienced a rather dramatic incident in my life that completely turned me around. It happened one afternoon as I was driving home during rush hour. I was bumper-to-bumpering on the freeway with the windows rolled up and the radio off—just me and my thoughts in my car.

A thought popped into my mind. Since the Lord has access to my thought life, I knew it was from Him. I was simply thinking of my wedding day and the site where I was married. I could picture that outdoor garden in my mind.

A second thought came into my mind. My wedding vows. Do you remember yours? Yours were probably like mine in that you promised your spouse everything, including the moon. You asked nothing for yourself, and you promised you would serve your spouse—words to that effect.

Then a third thought came crashing into my mind. It was in the form of a question: "Why, then, are you living a lie in your marriage instead of living out your vows?" Whoa—I didn't like that thought! It stung; I had no defense. Those ringing words in my head were all too true. I had done a 180-degree turn from the day of my wedding to where I was now. My promise of unselfish love to Yvonne was now one of selfish living on my part. What I had vowed to her before our Lord and many witnesses was nonexistent.

I felt angry with myself, and I felt shame. I also felt humbled before the Lord. As I continued driving home, tears formed in my eyes, and I softly said, "Yvonne, I'm sorry, and dear God, help me to resurrect my vows to be the husband You want me to be and whom Yvonne needs.

When I got home I didn't tell Yvonne what happened. As I went to bed that night I prayed, "Lord, help me to be obedient to your marching orders for me when I wake up in the morning."

The next morning my first conscious thought was "I am to be a godly husband and serve my wife, as Jesus came to serve me." So that day I focused on serving my wife's needs, not mine. It was that day I sensed the Lord telling me, as I now tell all husbands (and wives), "From this day forward, be God-centered and spouse-centered, no longer self-centered." I knew those were my marching orders for as long as I was married—to be a servant to my wife. After three days of faithfully focusing in this direction—

Yvonne: *I said, "What's wrong with you?" He was acting so different that I thought he was setting me up for something, because that's what he usually did. But this time I could tell he was genuinely different. He explained what had happened and where his heart and mind were now. I had been praying for years for something like this to occur. This was a major turning point for our marriage. Not overnight, but we progressed daily.*

About now you're probably asking, "What do I do to be a servant leader?" Good question. Here's where we get really practical, for there are three ways to live out a style of servant leadership: by being a protector, by being a provider, and by being a priest.

A Provider

The word "provide" means to get ready beforehand, to supply and furnish what is needed.

A servant leader doesn't do just what he wants but ob-
serves and decides what the needs of his mate and family are in
every situation. Look at what 1 Tim. 5:8 says: "If anyone does
not provide for his relatives, and *especially for his immediate family*, he has denied the faith and is worse than an unbeliever"
(emphasis added). With that verse in mind, let's now look at the
three key areas of this provision.

1. Provide for Her Financially

The husband must assume the main responsibility of hous-
ing, feeding, and clothing his family. This doesn't mean that his
wife can't or shouldn't work outside the home, but what it does
mean is that it is not her *responsibility* to provide for the family.
If she feels it's her responsibility, she starts to feel insecure in
the marriage.

As we talk with couples all across the country, we repeat-
edly see a certain situation that is causing a tremendous strain
on families. It's like Doug and Annette, a couple who've been
married for nearly five years. When they got married, they were
both working at well-paying jobs. They decided to buy a home,
new furniture, and two new cars that would take a major portion of both of their incomes. They figured they would get well
settled before the children arrived—but surprise! The first baby
"unexpectedly" arrived just after their second anniversary. At
first Annette figured she would go back to work after her six-
week maternity leave, but after the baby arrived she didn't
want to go back to work. She wanted to be a full-time stay-at-
home mom, but she had no choice in this matter as their
lifestyle was dependent upon her working full time. Unhappy,
she felt trapped. In only a matter of months she started to resent
her husband because she felt he was dependent upon her to
provide for the family. She even started to dislike her big house
they loved so much.

Annette would work all day, come home at night to care for
the baby, and take charge of all the many household responsibilities. She had zero time for herself or for Doug. She was just
plain worn out. Doug was feeling neglected since they didn't
have time for each other, and it seemed Annette was always
crabby. Instead of working together as a team, they were working against each other. What happened here is that Annette was

assuming the role of provider along with her husband, and now she didn't like it.

We often recommend that a couple in the beginning stages of their marriage build their lifestyle on the basis of his income and use her income for savings, vacations, extras, and so on. Then when children arrive, the decision on whether to go back to work is not based on the "she *has* to" syndrome. We continually hear from women that they have resentment if their salaries have to go to pay basic living expenses. The wife then doesn't feel she has any options if she wants to decide to quit her job and stay home with the children. Husbands, make sure, make *doubly* sure, you never put your wife in this position.

Yes, it may mean you have to rethink your lifestyle. A couple of areas in which some stressed-out couples have made some changes include

- Downsizing their home.
- Switching to buying used cars instead of always buying new ones.
- Looking at ways to upgrade the husband's skills to receive an advancement.
- Cutting back on eating out at restaurants.

There are many possibilities, but you have to be willing to make changes.

To lead by being the provider, the husband needs to ask himself, "Have I put my wife in the position of being a provider for the family? Have I been financially responsible? Are we in debt because of my spending money irresponsibly or my allowing other family members to do likewise? Have I forced my wife to go to work because I don't want to work so hard?"

We know of some men who, instead of working full-time jobs, took on only part-time ones. Since that covered only a portion of the bills, the wife *had* to become employed. Men, you need to make sure you're providing for your family in a way that will *reduce* stress on everyone instead of *increase* stress.

2. Provide for Her Future

Men, you need to talk to your wife about the vision you have for your future together, the direction in which you desire the family to go. In a later chapter we'll be giving you a plan to help you develop that vision.

Make sure you have adequate insurance on your personal property and on your life so that if the unexpected occurs, a major financial burden won't drop in on your family.

Make sure the two of you have drawn up a will or a living trust. If you haven't done so yet, don't delay any longer. Often younger couples don't want to be bothered with this discussion, or they figure it's for *older* couples. Listen—none of us knows how long our earthly life will be. That's an open end. Tragedies occur constantly. By preparing all these areas early in your marriage, it will make your wife feel loved and secure. And if you're in the child-rearing years, you need to plan all these areas for the sake of your children should something unforeseen happen to you both. You don't want the courts to decide who will raise your precious children, do you?

Yvonne: *Bob initiated something with me that demonstrated his love and care for me. He made up a written plan of what to do if anything should happen to either one of us. The plan clearly shows the location of all our important papers, people to call, arrangements that need to be made, and so on. Even though we worked together on this, Bob took the initiative to set it up instead of me even having to suggest it to him, or worse, nag him to do this for me. I personally felt this was a wonderful way of his demonstrating his leadership in our family, and it showed me he really cares about me.*

3. Provide for Her Growth

Do you know what your wife's dreams are? Have you even asked her? Are you helping her achieve them?

It could be that she wants to take night classes or pursue a hobby. This may mean providing the additional funds for her pursuits. It could be rearranging your own schedule to help her. Do you believe in your wife, and do you help her believe in herself? Do you help her become all that God desires for her?

What can greatly wound a wife is if comments like these are made to her: "My wife can't do much of anything" or "You'll never be able to do that. You're not capable enough."

Those words should be turned around to sound like this: "My wife can do just about anything she sets her mind to" and "Honey, give it a go. You're very capable."

Yvonne: *Bob is a tremendous encouragement to me and is the self-appointed president of my fan club. He saw abilities and talents in* *me that I never recognized. I would not be doing what I am today if my husband had not been there for me. It's wonderful to have a husband who really believes in me. It puts a happy smile on my face.*

A Protector

The word "protector" means one who shields another from injury, danger, or loss—a guard, a defender.

This paints a picture of what our Lord is to us: our shield. Ps. 28:7 says, "The LORD is my strength and my shield; my heart trusts in him, and I am helped." Your wife will trust you all the more when you demonstrate your servant leadership by being her protector. Here are a few ways you can be her protector.

1. Protect Her from Physical Harm

Make sure your cars are always in good running order. Weekly check the oil, tires, brake fluid, and so on. Keep the windows clean. Be sure you are both paid-up members of an auto club. Should she have to be out alone at night, see that she has a cellular phone with her in case of an emergency. Each night before bedtime, make sure the house is locked and secure.

Yvonne: *Ever since we were first married, Bob would have me role-play with him different scenarios that could possibly occur when I'm out and about by myself. This helped prepare me for the unexpected so I wouldn't be caught off guard. It has come in handy on more than one occasion. Once I was approached in a grocery store parking lot by a man and a woman who asked me for help with their car. Keep in mind that we live in a large metropolitan area where crime is always a concern. I thought it rather strange that they approached me when there were men close by in the parking lot they could have asked. The way they asked me sounded peculiar. I declined and started to return to the store to see the manager. As I got near the store entrance, I looked back, and they had just gotten back into their car and were speeding away. Because of my husband I was prepared.*

2. Protect Her from Too Much Pressure

Help your wife avoid becoming overcommitted or overscheduled. She can become fatigued more easily than you can. Help her say no to too many responsibilities. Make sure she has time for herself, whether it's to exercise, enjoy a hobby, or have a half-day or day to herself. Remember: she's always giving out and needs to be regenerated herself.

Seek to better understand what she does and what she struggles with. As you know, holiday time comes around faster every year, so when it hits, what are all the things she's juggling, and how can you help?

If your wife works outside the home, learn what her pressures are as she seeks to balance home and work. If she's home with young children all day, try to understand her strong need for adult conversation at the end of the day, and be prepared to give it to her.

When the kids become adults and leave home, be with her as she grapples with the empty-nest syndrome. Discuss with her and pray with her how you two are going to handle the years still ahead of you.

3. Protect Her from Family Pressures

One of the greatest ways to serve your wife is to be committed to playing an active role in the lives of your children and not taking the attitude that it's her job. Do you spend time reading to them, taking them on outings, playing games and sports with them, putting them to bed at night, teaching them life's lessons?

Twenty-six-year-old Trudie, who has a two-and-a-half-year-old son, sums it up for many moms when she says, "When my husband is always too busy to spend time with our son, just enjoying him, I take it as a message that he doesn't care about me either, since that child is part of me."

Don't neglect the gift of family that God has given you. Barbara Bush, wife of former United States President George Bush, said, "As important as your obligation as a doctor, a lawyer, or a business leader may be, your human connections with your spouse, your children, and your friends are the most important investments you will ever make. At the end of your life, you will never regret not having passed one more test, not winning one more verdict, or not closing one more deal. But you *will* regret time not spent with your spouse, your children, or your friends."

Bob: *Make sure your children treat their mother with respect. Most kids, especially boys, get to that certain age when they start* *smart-mouthing mom. Do not, repeat,* do not *let that occur. Instead of standing by the sidelines with a whimpering "Don't talk to your mother that way," step in between your wife and the offending child, look down at him or her straight in the eye, and say calmly but firmly, "Don't talk to my wife that way." When I said that to our son when he was about nine years old, he turned pale, gulped, mumbled, "Sorry," and slowly walked away. He later told me, "I suddenly realized that the person I was griping at was Dad's wife. I knew I was way out of line."*

Let your children know that you and your wife—their mom—are a team and that they are not to treat their mother disrespectfully—ever. And let them know that if they do, they'll have a big-time problem with you. However, to make this all really work, you have to make sure *you're* showing respect to your mate when you speak to her. Those little eyes and ears are watching and listening to you all the time. They are mini-tape recorders and cameras, and they see and hear everything. The way you treat your wife will play a big part in the way your daughter will want to be treated by the guys she dates. It will also impact your son in the way he treats the girls he dates, and it plants a seed as to how he'll treat his future wife as well.

4. *Protect Her by Being Honest with Her*

Bob: *One time when I was with the Honolulu Police Department, a criminal was so angry at me and two other men who helped put him behind bars that he vowed to get his revenge when he was released. It was long after I returned to the mainland from the 50th state that I received information from a former police department colleague that this man had been released and was heading for the mainland. And, yes, he was supposedly looking for me and one of the other two men who had also moved to the mainland. But that man had since died.*

I became very alert to the surroundings of my home and had a watchful eye for anyone walking or driving by my house who seemed suspicious to me. Yvonne's intuition told her something was wrong, but I downplayed it.

Finally, she became visibly upset, and I had to set her down to explain the situation. When the air was cleared, she felt greatly relieved and expressed her thanks to me for taking her into my confidence, but she also scolded me for not being up-front with her to begin with, which had caused needless anxiety in her. After she knew the facts, she felt more secure and able to work with me as a team in this possible threat.

The good news is that the man moved to the East Coast and evidently had quite a lifestyle change. Word filtered back to me that he had a wife, a solid marriage, and a good job, and that his anger has been mostly dispelled. Yvonne and I were both thankful for that. But I learned that being open with Yvonne made her feel more secure.

I think most men are like me. I don't want to tell Yvonne certain things because I don't want to upset or worry her. That's the protector shield we men wear. However, Yvonne is like most women—she's usually aware that something's up.

That's why being trustworthy is so important. Don't make her second-guess anything you're telling her. An example would be that you tell her you'll be home by 6:00, but you don't show up until 8:00. There were no phone calls in advance or any explanation when you walk in the door. You figure, "Well, I just got busy and forgot to call, and then after I got home, hey, I was home—so what's the big deal?" A wife feels secure when her husband makes a commitment, and then—and here's a novel idea—*he follows through with that commitment.*

A Priest

For many years women throughout the United States and Canada have told us that the main way to provide for them is for their husbands to give them spiritual leadership. A lack of it can bring disappointment. A case in point is the following letter we received from a woman who attended one of our marriage seminars in the state of Washington. What she wrote is indicative of many other women:

We enjoy a wonderful relationship as "best friends," "lovers," and all the other areas you both mentioned, but over the years our spiritual relationship has never grown, and sadly it has become very disappointing to me. I've been praying for my husband that he would become a spiritual leader. That he will do more than just sit in church and half listen to a sermon, but that God's Word will truly penetrate his life. I hunger for my husband to pray with me and help teach our children biblical principles. I share

everything with him but this one very important area of
my life. It makes me feel so lonely. It has become an area of
spiritual warfare in that I am tempted to resentment, dis-
trust, lack of respect, alienation in our physical relationship, and so on. Men need to know what a critical area this
is in their marriage.

Husband, do you pray with your wife? Do you study the
Bible with her? Do you attend church with her? Your main ministry is your wife, which means helping her grow spiritually.
You ask, "Does spiritual leadership mean that I have to initiate
everything and have superior knowledge about God and the Bible?" Of course not. But it does mean you set an atmosphere in
your home. That is what Joshua spoke about in Josh. 24:15,
when he said, "Choose for yourselves this day whom you will
serve . . . But as for me and my household, we will serve the
LORD."

Setting an atmosphere in the family is as simple as discern-
ing whether your wife feels free to share her feelings with you
without your putting her down. When she's worried, do you
dismiss or brush off her concerns and say things like "Ah,
c'mon. You shouldn't be so upset. That's just silly"?

Yvonne: *When I get uptight about a situation, Bob doesn't deliv-
er a sermon or quote scripture to me to make me feel guilty, but rather
he patiently listens. Then he will say, "Let's pray about this." To me,
that's demonstrating spiritual leadership.*

Being a servant leader is a way for your wife to feel secure
in the marriage. But there's something equally important that
your wife needs—something that can transform your wife.
Read on.

Team-Building Questions

1. As you started this chapter and it spoke about your being a leader,
   what characteristics came to your mind? Were they the same ones
   listed later in the chapter?
2. If you were to ask your wife which type of leader she thinks you are,
   would she say dictator, passive husband, or servant leader? If you
   have not been leading her, why not?
3. When you don't lead your wife, how does your wife deal with it?
4. Have you tried to be a spiritual leader? Has it been successful? Have

you experienced any problems in praying with your wife or having devotions together? If you haven't tried either, what are the things that have stopped you from doing them?

Team-Building Action Steps

1. List one practical thing you can do to be your wife's

provider _____

protector _____

priest _____

2. To help you with the list above, you may want to ask yourself some of the following questions—
Does she need encouragement?
Does she need help with a decision she's trying to make?
Does she need some time to herself?
Am I putting pressure on her for things I should be doing?
Do I help with the housework, the kids, and so on?

Father, thank You for making my wife
the type of woman I need in order
to become the type of man You want me to be.
Help me to be a servant leader.
In Jesus' name. Amen.

4

The Power of Loving Your Wife

Team Building Through Love

Husbands, love your wives,
just as Christ loved the church
and gave himself up for her.
—Eph. 5:25

*A*s a husband, do you know that it's within your ability to transform your wife? It's true. You have the ability to affect her actions, attitudes, and sense of self-worth. You have the ability to help her become the woman that God desires her to be. How? Through the power of your love. But here's the key—it's loving her in the same manner as Christ loves His Church. Yes, that's serious stuff, but read on.

The basis for that love is found in Eph. 5:25-30: "Husbands, love your wives, just as Christ loved the church and gave himself up for her to make her holy, cleansing her by the washing with water through the word, and to present her to himself as a radiant church, without stain or wrinkle or any other blemish, but holy and blameless. In this same way, husbands ought to love their wives as their own bodies. He who loves his wife loves himself. After all, no one ever hated his own body, but he feeds and cares for it, just as Christ does the church—for we are members of his body."

Looking at those verses, you'll find there are three important qualities of that love that can be translated into your own marriage. The first quality is *sacrifice* (v. 25). That's the same type of love Christ has for us. He loved us enough to die for us even when we were not deserving of that type of love. The biblical love spoken about here is not defined as an emotion or a feeling. It's an act of selfless sacrifice. That means you treat your wife in a loving way not only when you feel like it or when she acts in a deserving way. Instead, it's acting in love when she has a need, in spite of your feelings. Take for instance when she gets off the phone all in tears over something going on in her mother's life, and she needs to talk to you about it right then. But you're right in the middle of the fourth quarter of the USC-UCLA football game, so you give her the brush off and say, "Hang on, Babe. I'll talk to you after the Trojans flatten the Bruins." That's not loving her with a sacrificial love. However, if it's near the end of a tied Super Bowl game—well, that might be negotiable. Seriously, aren't you glad when you cry out to your Heavenly Father in *your* hour of need that you don't get an answering machine or get put on hold?

Your love for your wife is to be a purifying love (vv. 26-27). Christ cleanses His Church by forgiving us of our sins when we come to Him for salvation, and through sanctifying grace He continues building a holy people.

Purifying your wife so she is without blemish means making sure you don't neglect her needs. If you do neglect her needs, it could cause her to sin should she look to someone else for the fulfillment of those needs.

Your love is to be a caring love (vv. 28-30). Christ cares for His Church. He supplies everything we need, whether it's love, joy, strength, wisdom—anything. That's a promise we're given in Phil. 4:19: "My God will meet all your needs according to his glorious riches in Christ Jesus." You're God's agent to meet your wife's needs. Our verses in Eph. 5 also say you're to feed and care for your wife as you do your own body. The one word that explains how a man cares for his body is the word "constant." No man would ever say, "Wow—that was a delicious meal, but I don't think I'll eat again for three years." In a matter of hours he's looking forward to his next meal, because his body needs food continually. This constant care should be the same in expressing love to your wife.

If you were to say, "Let's see—I remembered her on our anniversary last month. Gave her some flowers and a card, took her to dinner, and told her I loved her. Good—that should hold her until our next anniversary." Not good thinking.

Your wife needs a lot more than an annual nod in her direction. She needs your love and attention daily, even hourly. If you demonstrate your love constantly, it will fend off remarks such as *"Now* what do you want?" or *"Now* what have you been up to?" Such remarks would be an indication that you have been demonstrating love only when you want something. That's not caring love. Trust us—those kinds of remarks will end when you give her the constant love and attention she needs and deserves.

You are to love your wife in an understanding way (1 Pet. 3:7). That means you need to understand her so you'll know how to meet her needs.

Right now you're probably thinking, "That's why I'm reading this book—to better understand her, because at times she's really hard to understand."

For example, I've noticed that even though my wife and I are both speaking American English, somehow our translations are different—as when she says to me, "Well, OK"—that really means "No." Or if she says, "No, I don't think so," it means "Yes." Or "We need . . ." really means "I want . . ." Or "No, I'm not upset" means "Of course I'm upset—you should know that." Or "I'm not yelling!" means "Yes, I *am* yelling because I think this is important!" And, of course, the mysterious answer to the question "What's wrong?" If she answers, "The same old thing," that means nothing. But if she answers, "Nothing," that means *everything.* And don't forget: if she says, "Everything is the matter," that means "My PMS is acting up." See what I mean? She *is* complex.

Yes, that's why it takes your understanding to know how to love her in the way she desires. We've found that it isn't so much that a husband doesn't want to meet his wife's needs— it's that often he just doesn't know how. Ring true for you?

Bob: *For years I couldn't seem to read Yvonne correctly. I just assumed her needs were the same as mine. Like the time she was coming up on a major transition birthday: she said to me, "Honey, don't do anything for me on my birthday." So, being a guy, I took her liter-*

ally and did nothing for her, save a birthday card.

Yvonne: *When I said, "Don't do anything," I didn't mean any-thing. (Remember what we just said about different translations?) I just meant, "Don't go to a big fuss" as he had done in the past. I meant, "Let's do this birthday in a more subdued manner."*

Bob: *Wow—did I miss the mark on that one!*

We're going to help you understand your wife a little bit better by looking at four keys that can unlock the mystery of loving her in a way that speaks love to her. We'll give you the overriding principles plus some practical ideas, but you need to become a detective of your wife so you'll know how to live out these keys the way she would like.

Bob Takes It from Here

Now Bob will be the writer because of how we conduct a particular session in our seminar. We separate men and women, and Bob teaches the wives how to love their husbands while Yvonne teaches the husbands how to love their wives. Through teaching the women, Bob continually hears the women say, "Our husbands just don't understand what we need. Would you please tell them?" So now is Bob's opportunity to give men the scoop from the ladies themselves.

Key No. 1—Time

Your wife's world revolves around relationships—develop-ing, nurturing, and sustaining those relationships. Ever since she made her first eye contact soon after birth, she has been more interested in people than in things. The relationship that has the greatest importance to her is the one she has with you, her husband. Your wife wants to be a vital part of your life. She wants to be your partner. She wants and needs your time and attention.

Think back to those earlier times when you were first get-ting to know each other—when you had, if you'll pardon a '60s expression, those *vibes* for her. You did anything and everything to get and keep her attention. You would do special little things for her. You would blow a whole paycheck on a date with her. But hey—it was well worth it. Besides, ketchup and crackers made a great meal the next night when you ate at home alone. You would go out of your way to find the type of flowers she loves. You didn't even notice how sleep-deprived you were, because you were anxious to spend all your waking hours with her. You would talk endlessly with her about your goals.

At first she was probably thinking, "This guy is too good to be true." After a while with your persistent way, you won her heart. As she was walking down the wedding aisle, she was likely thinking, "This man I'm marrying is the greatest man on this earth. He spends so much time with me and makes me feel so special with all his attention. I just know he'll be the same way the rest of my married life."

Yeah, right! What happened? As you were walking down the aisle, *you* were thinking, "I did it! I conquered her! I accomplished my goal of having her become my wife. I love that woman, and right after the honeymoon I'm going to go on to my next goal—my career."

Do you see how these two ways of thinking could cause a problem? She enjoys the ongoing process of having a relationship. It isn't a goal to be conquered. She wants you to think that there isn't anything more important in life than giving her attention and spending time with her. When you do that, you're telling her that she's important, special. It's part of making her a priority in your life.

I used to tell Yvonne all the time that she was a priority in my life. But she would continually say to me, "If that's true, how come I feel I'm always getting your leftovers?" She said I spent time with her only when I was exhausted from a long day of giving out to everyone else. To her, it looked as though the last thing I wanted to give her was the time and attention she needed.

Another problem area in our relationship was the phone calls during the dinner hour. Dinnertime was family time for us, a time for everyone to connect. But the phone always seemed to ring at that time. I would answer it and spend the dinner hour attending to someone else's needs. When I arrived back at the table after dinner, Yvonne would ask me, "Couldn't you tell the caller that you'd phone them after your dinner?"

But I would usually say, "What I'm doing is important, and they needed me right then. You do know, don't you, that I'm doing God's work? Do you want me to stop that?" Yvonne felt she couldn't say anything—otherwise she would be fighting God. What I didn't realize was that I was telling Yvonne, without saying it, that she wasn't as important as those nightly calls.

What I found out in our marriage was that over a period of time everything became a threat to her, whether it was phone calls from others, conversations I had, watching or coaching football, reading the newspaper—just about anything and everything. Each of those things represented time and attention taken from her. She was hurt, and the way she showed it was by complaining about everything I would do. When that occurred, I would then retreat from her, which caused more complaining from her and further retreat from me. We were in this vicious cycle. Now, from my perspective I didn't intentionally neglect her need for attention and time. I was just so busy with meeting the needs of many others that I figured she would understand. Plus I figured I would attend to her later since her needs didn't seem so immediate. In other words, I did what so many other men have done to their wives: I took her for granted. It took me a long time to see that her needs were important and that I needed to treat her as a priority and not just do it with words only.

I realized that I was not loving Yvonne in the way the Lord had commanded me to. When I read what Matt. 6:21 said, I began to realize my comment to Yvonne about her being a priority was ringing hollow. That biblical verse convicted me: "Where your treasure is, there your heart will be also." I had been placing my treasure in everything but her. I knew in my position of servant leadership that I needed to humble myself before her and ask for forgiveness. This started to break the vicious cycle we were in. Since that time I have discovered the things that make Yvonne feel like a priority, and I do them. What a difference it has made in our marriage! But here's the kicker: Do you remember that I said Yvonne felt threatened by everything and because of that she would complain about anything I wanted to do? When she started seeing that she was once again a priority in my life as a result of my actions, she no longer felt threatened. We became teammates, and she helped me do the things I had wanted to do instead of battling me the whole way. What a difference when you give your wife the time and attention she so craves!

Guys, focus all the more on this next part. Making your wife a priority in your life is more than just being in her presence. It is your *attitude* when you're spending time with her that lets her know if she really is a priority to you. An example is as follows.

Susie was so excited. She and her husband were going out to eat at a nice restaurant. She looked forward to it all day, picked out a special outfit, took extra time fixing her makeup and hair. She thought, "We're going to spend time together— just the two of us and no kids. I feel special."

When they got to the restaurant, Susie mused, "Just what I wanted. Lights are low, soft music playing. Just the right atmosphere to have a nice leisurely dinner together. A time just to enjoy each other. I'm so happy."

After they were seated, Susie started to talk to her husband, Jeff. Unfortunately, his nose was in the menu and he was busy studying it, so he gave off only a few grunts to Susie. Since she kept talking, in exasperation he put the menu down, glanced at her, and said, "I thought we came here to eat. Will you please stop talking and look at the menu?"

Now Susie felt a bit sad.

They ordered the food and it arrived fairly quickly. As they started to eat, Susie decided to try again with conversation. She thought, "It's so nice not being interrupted by the kids every few words." Then she noticed Jeff wolfing his food down, so she said lightheartedly, "Honey, you sure must be hungry. Maybe you'd better slow down a bit—you'll be finished before I even eat my salad."

At that he exploded and said, "Look—I didn't want to come here in the first place! It was all your idea! You know I want to watch the game tonight, so will you hurry up?"

They ate the rest of their dinner in silence. Susie barely touched her meal, but Jeff didn't even seem to notice. Then they left so he could get home to spend time with the TV set. Susie's thought when they arrived home was "I guess I'm just not important."

Jeff assumed that by simply taking Susie out to eat, she would be happy. But Susie didn't go out for the food as much as for the experience of spending some quality time with her husband. She was hoping he would just enjoy being with her. But he indicated in every way that she wasn't important and that he preferred being somewhere else.

Susie is not the only woman hurt by such situations. Your wife wants to think you can't wait to be with her. That's what it means to make her a priority. In other words,

- Don't make her compete for your attention with work, hobbies, the computer, sports, and the like. She'll always feel she's losing.
- Ask her to write down five ways that you can make her feel like a priority. Then put them into action. Also, think constantly of new ways to make her feel special.
- Mark special times with her on your calendar and put them *in ink.*
- When you're with her, *be there.* Don't think about all the work you need to do or other things you want to do. Focus on her. This makes her feel loved.

Key No. 2—Talk

For a wife, conversation is the glue that binds her together with her husband. It's her way of feeling close to you, to feel connected. That's why you may have had a scenario like this with her:

You come home from work, mumble a few words as you walk into the house, kind of scrunch your head near hers to give her a kiss that misses her mouth by five inches, and then proceed to plop down in front of the television set while reading the sports or business section of the newspaper. After a quiet dinner with little conversation, you zone out in front of your computer the rest of the evening. Again, little or no conversation. Then just before bedtime, she walks past you in her nightie, you do a double take, and *shazam*—you suddenly come alive, and that gleam in your eye appears. So you make your lover-boy move and approach her, and what does she say? "Don't touch me. You haven't even talked to me all night, and now you want *what?*" What she's saying, Tiger, is that she doesn't feel connected to you.

Yvonne used to say this to me, and I would quickly say, "OK—start talking. How long do you think it'll take?" I didn't understand it wasn't about how many minutes I had to talk in order to accomplish my goal. It was about the process of talking to share each other's lives.

It's not just talking on a level of facts, such as just repeating what happened "factually" during the day. It's most satisfying to her when you communicate on the *emotional* level. She is a people-centered person. She wants to share her inner thoughts and feelings with you and wants to know your dreams, your thoughts, your doubts, and yes, even your hurts. Easy? No way. It takes work and time, but it isn't impossible. But you have to start with the realization that a woman has a deep need to communicate with her husband. Listen to what two women have told me:

Maggie, age 36 and married 12 years, said, "My husband doesn't talk to me. He comes home from work and retreats to the TV set and newspaper immediately. He does this night after night. When I try to talk with him, most of the time I only get a grunt, an uh-huh, or a short answer like 'What's for dinner?' There are also times when all I get is dead silence. I don't know why he married me. All he really needs is a housekeeper and somebody to sleep with him when he's in the mood. Frankly, he could hire women for that. I just wish he could understand how much I desire to talk with him, to share our lives with each other. Doesn't he realize how much he's hurting me by not wanting to talk?"

Forty-four-year-old Bettie, married 22 years, told me, "The importance of talking to a woman? How well I know it! I had an affair with a man for 2 years. It didn't start out as a sexual encounter between the two of us. In fact, over the 2 years we had sex only about a dozen times. Our relationship was more about sharing ourselves with one another on a different level. The reason I felt I loved him is because he talked with me and actually listened to me. We would talk for hours, just enjoying each other. I could tell him anything that was on my heart, and he did the same with me. Even though the affair is over, I still long for our conversations. I only wish my husband and I could communicate the way my ex-lover and I did."

At this point some of you men may be thinking, "I know it's important. I don't disagree with you, but I don't know *how* to communicate with her. A lot of times I'm not even sure what she wants. Plus, we often end up in an argument, so why bother?" Or you might be thinking, "We just don't have time to communicate. It's not there. There are so many other pressing things that grab our time and attention."

That's why you're reading this book, right? Communication is such an important part of a marital relationship, especially for women. Read on.

Praise Her

An important part of talk for a woman is when she's on the receiving end of praise. A most pressing problem for women nowadays is low self-image. Many women don't feel what they do or who they are has value.

Recently we saw a list of all the different hats a wife wears these days. Just a few of them are cook, nurse, counselor, teacher, wardrobe consultant, chauffeur, maid, schedule planner, interior decorator, bill-payer, partner, lover, hostess, volunteer, friend, and church member. She doesn't get paid for these, of course, but the biggest payment her husband can give her is praise.

As a husband, notice all that your wife does, and praise her. That lets her know you don't take for granted what she does. The children usually expect these from Mom and often forget to thank her, but please—don't *you* overlook them. Let her know you and the family wouldn't be where all of you are today if it weren't for her. Let her know that she's important. Let her know that she's valued. It makes all she does worthwhile to her when you express to her your appreciation.

In the Bible, praise of God is a natural response to enjoying God. Do you enjoy your wife? Then praise her. Prov. 31:28 says, "Her children arise and call her blessed; her husband also, and he praises her." A wife receiving this will be a satisfied wife.

You ask, "What do I praise her about?"

Well, for starters, when she's looking especially good, let her know it. I remember one time we were going somewhere and Yvonne was running late. I was already in the car as she came running into the garage to get in. At that moment I realized I hadn't even noticed her, since I was so focused on getting to the event. So Yvonne just stood in front of the car, with her hands on her hips, waiting for a compliment. All she got was my yelling, "Hurry up and jump in the car! We're going to be late!" That wasn't about to keep her from making her point, so she just stood there smiling at me.

It quickly dawned on me what she was pulling, so this time I yelled, "You're lookin' like a fox, Honey! Now come on and jump in the car!" That was all she needed, so she laughed and jumped in. I could see that I often get focused somewhere else and forget to notice her and all the many wonderful things she does. I learned I have to be more intentional in my praise, to observe such things and let her know.

There are so many more things you can praise your wife for, the way she takes care of the house; her cooking (if she cooks); her laugh; her smile; her kisses; the way she handles the children; her work; what a good friend she is to you and others; her honesty; how wonderful she is with your parents; how she remembers others' birthdays . . . well, the list is endless. It could sound like this: "Thanks for matching all my socks in my drawer." "You look mighty good to me when I come home from work." "You're a great wife and mom." "I appreciate you always being there for me." "It means so much to me to know that you love me and are always praying for me." Just open your eyes to those areas of praise available to you. There are many.

One man told us something he does every day to help him remember to give compliments to his wife. He puts five coins in his right pocket as a reminder to give his wife at least five compliments that day. Then when he gives her one, he'll switch a coin from the right to the left pocket. At the end of the day he'll check his left pocket to make sure he accomplished his goal. That's creative. Do whatever it takes to trigger your memory, but the main point is to do something.

Now you probably realize that if you start giving your wife compliments and you haven't been doing it in the past, you might get the reaction that evangelist Billy Sunday mentioned: "Try praising your wife, even if it does frighten her at first." If she does go into a near faint, that will only prove that you haven't been doing it enough. Keep it up, and her fainting spells will end.

Another way to praise her is to brag about her. "My wife makes the *best* Swedish pancakes" or "My wife knows a lot about that subject—she could give you some good insight about it" or "As busy as she is, my wife takes the time to take care of herself. She looks great, and that's inspired me to want to do the same." Any of these give you some helpful ideas of your own?

Before my wife started exercising at the same gym I was going to, the various people I got acquainted with soon learned I was married and heard me talk about Yvonne.

Yvonne: *Bob said so many nice things about me to everyone that when I finally arrived, people would say, "Oh, your husband has spoken so highly of you!" That really pleased me. Another area that pleases me is to know that over the years Bob has often told my parents how much he appreciates me. That pleases them too, and it sure helps me know that he loves me.*

Well, I do love Yvonne, so it's easy to rave about her. Speaking of love, husband, tell your wife *often* that you love her. Sometimes we guys get so focused on other things that we forget how important hearing those words are to her. Don't be like the man who told his wife, "Listen—when I married you 31 years ago I told you I loved you and that if I ever changed my mind I would let you know." That's hardly what she wants or needs. It's a fact that she can't hear you say "I love you" often enough. But if you haven't been saying those words enough and she has to ask you, "Do you love me?" the best answer is "Yes, I certainly do." The wrong answer to this question could get you in real trouble. Some examples of the wrong answers are

"I suppose so."

"Would it make you feel better if I said yes?"

"That depends on what you mean by 'love.'"

"Does it matter?"

These will not score high on her love meter. In fact, you will have just struck out.

Key No. 3—Tenderness

What's this tenderness stuff all about? Read what former United States President Theodore Roosevelt wrote in his journal the day his wife accepted his marriage proposal: "The aim of my whole life shall be to make her happy and to shield her and guard her from every trial; and, oh, how I shall cherish my sweet queen. How one so pure and sweet and beautiful can think of marrying me, I cannot understand, but I praise and thank God it is so."

Another president of the United States, Harry Truman, wrote his wife, Bess, hundreds of love letters throughout their married life. Now maybe you're thinking, "Oh, sure—now you're telling me I have to start writing love letters. Great!" No, I'm not telling you to do anything. But if this is something your wife has really wanted and you keep telling her you can't, then you don't believe Phil. 4:13: "I can do *everything* through him who gives me strength" (emphasis added). That is *everything*, even writing a love letter to your wife. If I can do it, you can do it. Yvonne had been asking me to write her one for years, but I kept putting her off—until last Christmas. I decided I was going to give it to her as a holiday gift. Unfortunately, I put it off until the day before Christmas, and I hadn't penned the words yet. I prayed and asked God to give me the words as I sat down to write it. This is what I gave her at Christmas. (We flipped a coin on whether I would put this in our book. She won the toss.)

1997 Christmas Thoughts for My Yvonne
from her loving and thankful husband

Within our beautiful home we have many wonderful
"things," but the best thing in our home is you!
You are my best friend, and my desire is that this coming year
I praise you more—in the way that would please God.
Many times you've heard me say, "You're a good wife." That
means you are God's good gift to me.
How much dearer you are these many years as my wife than
even when you were first my bride!
You are my faithful wife, which causes me many
thanksgivings, and you are a source of joy.
There is nothing—nada, zippo, zilch—NOTHING upon this
earth that can be compared to you.
Being my good wife makes the cares and concerns of this
world sit easier for me.
If you weren't my wife, I would be living in a world devoid
of a sun.
Next to Jesus, you are God's greatest gift bestowed upon me.
Heaven will be great, no question, and it will be all the
better because you'll be there.
I love you, my beloved. Merry and blessed Christmas to you!

When Yvonne read the words on Christmas she started crying, and my mother, who was with us, also started crying. We were having a happy cry-a-thon. Both of them thought it was so special. In fact, Yvonne has it framed and hung up for her to glance at any time. She said it showed her how much I cared for her to do something that was not easy for me.

Writing a love letter may not hit your wife's love button, but that's not the point. It's finding out what pleases her and doing those *little* things that let her know you're thinking about her. Keep in mind that she's giving out continually to meet everyone else's needs. Expressing tenderness to her is a way she can sit back and receive. It revitalizes her so she then can give out again.

In a moment you'll read some ideas about tenderness, and I don't want you men to totally go into your "logic" mode. We guys use logic when dealing with just about anything. We've even learned to trust in our logic, especially when it shows us something will work over and over again. We figure, "Hey—if it works, let's don't change it and try something new."

Example: A husband comes home and surprises his wife with some flowers. She reacts with excitement. He figures that was such a good response that he'll do the same thing next week. Again, she's happy, but this time not excited. Third week—no excitement as she takes the flowers, but she does thank him. He's thinking, "I can't seem to please her, so why try?"

She's thinking, "That was nice, but if he's going to do something like this for me, it would be nice for him to think of different things to do instead of just repeating the same thing."

Men like consistency. Women like change. And women also like variety. A husband needs to demonstrate his tenderness in many different ways, not just one way only, repeated over and over.

Be careful also not to take the attitude that "If she wants something, all she has to do is ask and I'll do it." For a woman that doesn't cut it. If she has to ask you to buy her flowers and you go out and buy them, she won't be very excited about them. This makes her feel like a beggar. She doesn't want to beg for your love and attention. Work as a team on this, as with one couple we know. If her husband hasn't purchased her flowers in a while and she would like him to remember her that way, she puts an empty vase next to the front door. That's his clue to do something about it. It works for both of them.

Now read on for some ideas on expressing tenderness.

Daily

Ask yourself daily, "What can I do today that will demonstrate to my wife that I love her and I'm thinking about her?"

Here are some things I do for Yvonne: making sure our car is never less than half full of gas, taking out the trash every night, putting paper in her computer printer so she doesn't run out while working, making sure the roll of toilet paper is never left empty, turning on her electric blanket before she gets into bed during our so-called southern California winter, staying in good physical shape for her, and always smelling clean. Those are just a few of the little ways I try to make her feel special and loved.

Here are a few more ideas for you to consider:

- Call her at work to say, "Hi, Hon. Love ya."
- Finish the laundry for her even though she didn't ask.
- Send flowers periodically to her workplace or bring them home after work.
- Fix something in the house that needs it, without being asked.
- Shock her by saying, "Let's turn off the TV *and talk.*"
- Bring her a cup of coffee into the bedroom in the morning.
- On a Saturday, let her sleep in and *you* take care of the kids.
- Clean the bathroom(s)—and don't forget the toilet(s).
- Always treat her as a lady by extending to her common courtesies—opening the car door, pulling out the chair for her, saying, "Please" and "Thank you."

Special Occasions

Always remember those special occasions in her life like anniversaries, birthdays (hers and the kids'), Valentine's Day, Christmas, and so on. Some of these times may not mean all that much to you, but they certainly do to her, and being a loving servant leader means you're wanting to do things that mean something to her. You can remember her with a card or a gift or a night out on the town.

We said *card.* Have you noticed that women love cards? Words on cards mean a lot to her. Women spend a lot of time in a card shop, reading them and then picking out just the right one. When she buys a card for her husband, he reads it, thanks her for it, and then probably within two hours it's in his waste-basket. Nothing rude. It's just that he has read it.

Not her. She may display the card for a couple of weeks and look at it and read it many times over. Then she fondly places the card in her memory box to reread periodically.

I never used to take the time to pick out a card because I never realized the words meant that much to Yvonne. I learned my lesson when one time I was in such a hurry I grabbed a card that looked OK for the occasion, but I didn't take time to read the inside of it. It was for a wife having a baby. When Yvonne read the card she said, "This is news to *me!*"

Another thing I do for Yvonne that's always a surprise and a delight for her is to buy a bunch of cards and place one of them under her bed pillow when she least expects it, so that when she goes to bed at night she finds it. I've learned that this speaks tenderness to her, and it tells her I was thinking about her.

Here's a thought on giving your wife a gift. Do not, I repeat, do *not* buy her anything that plugs in. That's much too practical. The gift you give her signifies what you think of her.

A pastor friend of ours learned about practical gifts the hard way. He and his wife have a summer house a few hours away from their home. They decided to spend Christmas at this home away from home that is located in snow country. All their children and grandchildren would be coming for the holidays. The husband was concerned because the house didn't have indoor plumbing and his wife would have to trudge out in the snow to use the outhouse. So he thought the best gift he could give his wife would be a port-a-potty. He purchased it, wrapped it, and placed it under their Christmas tree. With all the family watching, she opened the port-a-potty present on Christmas morn. Do you think she was a happy camper? You got it! He quickly realized he goofed in trying to pass this off as a *gift* and that he should have simply bought the port-a-potty for her another time and had something *special* under the tree.

With gift-giving it isn't always the cost or the size of the gift that brings her delight. It is more or less whether you thought about her or didn't think about her in the process of getting the gift. There used to be a radio commercial in our area by a local florist who advertised to the men listeners that "I'll take care of all your floral needs. Give me the dates of special occasions for your wife, and I'll see that flowers go out on those dates."

The men loved this pitch because they would be assured of never forgetting the occasion. But from a woman's point of view that ad didn't fly, especially if she had to pay the charge card bill. What she might say is, "You thought about me once and only once when you set this up. I want to know you're thinking about me all the time."

Just Because

This is doing something for your mate or giving her something not because it's a special occasion, but "just because I love you."

- Plan a getaway weekend. Take care of all the arrangements—even getting the baby-sitter for the kids.
- Go for a walk after dinner, hold hands, and talk.
- Throw a surprise "unbirthday" party. I did this for Yvonne recently. Her birthday is in September, but I put together a party for her in January. She had been working long hours for months, and I felt she needed something to make her feel special. It was a complete surprise, and yes, it was enjoyable for me to see Yvonne enjoy herself so much, surrounded by many friends.
- Periodically give her the day off. *You* take care of the children and house and meals, and she can do whatever she wants.
- Leave her little notes around the house telling her you love her.

Don't overlook the opportunities to do little things for her. Don't be like the man who mourned over his wife's coffin. When she was alive he was always too busy to buy her gifts, take her out on a date, even buy her flowers. She died unexpectedly, and at the funeral he was asked to place some roses on her coffin. As he did so he wept, realizing he was *finally* giving her flowers, but now it was too late for her to enjoy them.

Key No. 4—Touch

I now hear you guys shouting, "All right, Bob. We knew you'd come through for us. You're finally getting to the good stuff—touching." Sorry to disappoint you, but I'm not talking about sex. I'm talking about a new English word for your vocabulary. It's brand-new. Ready for this one? *Affection.*

Affection to a woman sends messages of protection and se-curity. It says, "I care about you and your needs."

Jodie was having one of those "pit" days, when the kids seemed out of control and just about everything that day was going wrong. When Mike walked through the door at 6:30 that evening, she unloaded on him the details of her day. Jodie said, "He listened to me, then pulled me into his arms and held me for a couple of minutes. Just being in his arms lowered my stress level and made me feel secure. His touch was the special turning point for me. Mike then told me he would feed the kids and play with them while I went and took a relaxing bath. Then he put them to bed so we could have a dinner together. I felt loved and I felt protected." *That's* affection.

What I often hear from women is that their husbands don't understand their strong need for continual affection. The hugs, kisses, pats, hand-holding, arm around her, sitting close on the couch, snuggling in bed; courteous gestures like opening car doors, pulling chairs out, helping her with her coat. Right now, as a man, think about your strong desire and need for sex. You don't have to dwell on that for too long. Guess what—that same intensity you feel is what she feels about her need for affection. Yes, it's that strong.

Another question I often receive when I'm doing the for-women-only session at one of our marriage conferences is "Why don't husbands understand that we wives enjoy affection just for what it is—affection?" They say their husbands seem to believe that affection has to always be linked to something. We know what that link is—sex. For years in my marriage I didn't understand the term "nonsexual touching." I didn't think you could have one without the other. Over a period of time I came to realize that Yvonne's emotional and physical parts are tightly connected. She cannot separate the two. That explains how we could have a disagreement, settle it, and the case is closed for me. Within a short period of time I would get what Yvonne calls "that gleam in my eyes" and start sexually approaching her.

I would hear Yvonne say to me, "How can you be ready to make love when we haven't even talked to one another since our disagreement? I need something like talk, some tenderness."

I didn't need that because I deal with life in compartments. I had been in the argument compartment, but since it was over with, I had closed the door. I didn't need to talk to get ready to jump into the next compartment, the sex compartment. I simply opened it up and was ready to go.

But I've learned that's not true with my wife. The sexual relationship is part of her whole relationship with me. She needs to be nurtured emotionally before she can successfully respond physically.

Men, we need to understand that our wives often just want affection without it being linked to sex. If the only time a husband gives his wife affection is because he's "going for the gold," meaning, of course, he wants sex with her, then after a while she'll start feeling she's being used, and in some cases misused. She wants and needs to know that you enjoy her company for who she is rather than for what pleasure she can give you.

It may mean we need to change a mind-set and look at affection as "the setting" and sex as "the event." The setting needs to be developed long before the event and then continued long after the event. A book that captures that spirit so well is written by Kevin Leman and titled *Sex Begins in the Kitchen*. Its premise is that we husbands need to set a whole atmosphere of caring and tenderness on a continual basis. It's all about how you greet her in the morning, the way you kiss and hug her, and the kind words before you separate for the day. It's about giving her a call during the day to tell her, "I'm thinking about you." It's about greeting her with a hug and a kiss when you see her in the evening. It's about connecting when you get home by sharing the day's activities with each other, helping with the kids or household chores or anything else that needs to be done. It's sitting next to her on the couch as you watch TV, paying attention to her, talking with her, touching her with no strings attached. And when there *is* a sexual encounter, it's the affection you display afterward—not turning your back and falling asleep. Nurture her emotionally.

When all or most of this is done, this creates the desire within her to express her love for you, and she'll respond to your sexual advances. If she isn't receiving her share of touch and tender-loving care, then her desire for sexual intimacy is one of the first things to diminish. But don't give her affection just so you can get something. That's being self-centered. Loving her with the same love Christ has for you—that's what will meet her needs. And that includes giving her affection.

Let me add this. There's a part of her anatomy that needs to be attended to if there's going to be any sexual intimacy. It's her nose. Fooled you. You can't bluff me—you thought I was going to say something different. Here's the point: make sure when you do approach her that you're *clean*. Very clean. Too many men work hard all day and then crawl into bed without a shower or even freshening up a bit. Her sense of smell is much more acute than yours, and it affects her desire level. She wants to know that you care enough about her to clean up.

With all this talk about affection, you may be thinking that fulfilling this need is going to be a difficult task. You're saying, "I don't know how to be affectionate. I didn't grow up in an affectionate family." OK, but affection can be learned. You can actually develop a habit of affection. At first you may need to humble yourself before your wife and ask her to help you learn how to be affectionate.

Years ago when I took my first baby steps in this arena, Yvonne appreciated my efforts and was very patient with me. She was there to cheer me on as I took my next steps. Over the years God has enabled me to come a long way from where I was to where I am today. I'm still learning and still growing, and her appreciation grows right along with me. He'll do the same for you. You just have to ask.

Final Thoughts

Hopefully in this chapter I have given you some insight into loving your wife in a way that meets her need for love by giving you the overarching principles with time, talk, tenderness, and touch.

It's now your job to know what your wife would like in each of those areas. Each woman is different in what she likes. Take Yvonne, for example. Her favorite flower is the rose. With her practical personality she has told me that I don't need to buy her a dozen roses—just a single rose will have the impact for her. Now if you think, "Hey—if it works for Bob I'm sure it will work for me," you could be headed for a disaster. First of all, your wife may not like roses, and second, she may be the type who likes a whole dozen, not just one. Be a detective. Get to know her likes and dislikes.

I've also mentioned loving your wife as Christ loves the Church—with a sacrificial, purifying, caring type of love. You can do this only if you die to self daily. When I mention dying to self, I often have guys say, "Yes, I'd give my life for my wife. If an out-of-control semi truck were barreling down a road heading for her, I'd throw my body at the truck while at the same time pushing her to safety. If a band of terrorists storm my house with automatic weapons, I'll take their opening salvo after seeing that my wife and children flee to safety." Applause, applause—but, will you "die for her" when it comes to doing something she enjoys? Maybe go shopping with her. (Yeah, I know—you'd rather get hit by the truck.)

When Yvonne would ask me to go to the store to try on some clothes she had already picked out, I often would go with an attitude that it was such a bother. I would let her know by my attitude that I felt I had much more important things to do than try on clothes. Then it dawned on me how selfish I was being. I cared only about my own time frame. I wasn't thinking that she was taking her time and effort to shop for me. I needed to die to self and let God renew me.

There will be moments, and even days, when you won't feel like it because so many things pull at you *not* to love her in the way she needs to be loved. A variety of things you read or watch will pull you in the direction of wanting to rule over your wife. And frankly, just your natural self is bent toward self-centeredness because of what happened as a result of the Fall in the Garden of Eden. That's the bad news.

The good news is that our Heavenly Father knows all this, and that's why He made a way possible for a man to lead and love his family through His power and strength. That's why the only way you will be successful in your role as husband is by having a growing relationship with Jesus Christ. A man who does this is a man who is seeking to find God's will instead of always relying on his own decisions. He's a man who finds and then follows God's way instead of always following his own methods. He is both dependent on God and confident in what God can do, instead of spending his energies being self-reliant and having confidence in only what he can do.

It takes quite a man to deny himself daily and then open himself to the Holy Spirit so the Spirit may empower him. Learning how to do this will take time, prayer, and help. Part of that help is being involved with a men's accountability group— a gathering of godly men learning together, holding one another accountable, and helping one another become the leaders God desires.

Is all this worth it? I answer you with a resounding yes!

Team-Building Questions

1. Have you been loving your wife in the same manner that Christ loves His Church? If not, what have been some of your roadblocks?
2. Right now how are you communicating to your spouse that she is special? Is there any room for improvement?
3. In what ways could you make a change in your schedule so you would have time to spend with her—time to talk, time for tenderness, and time for touch? Get her ideas on these as well.

Team-Building Action Steps

1. Your wife may know you love her, but she needs to see it in a tangible way and on an ongoing basis. Make a list of three ways under each area that will express love to her. Then express them to her consistently.

Time

_____

_____

_____

Talk

_____

_____

_____

Tenderness

_____

_____

_____

Touch

_____

_____

_____

2. Periodically write her a letter expressing your love. Here are some suggestions about what to include:
Why you enjoy her
What she does that you admire
What you appreciate about her
Ways you've seen her grow spiritually, emotionally, and so on
Why you love her so much

> *Father, thank You for loving me even when*
> *I'm so unlovable. Help me to learn what*
> *expressions of love mean the most to my wife,*
> *and give me the courage to put them into practice.*
> *In Jesus' name. Amen.*

5

How to Be a Champion of a Wife

TEAM BUILDING THROUGH THE WIFE'S ROLE

If you treat a man as he is, he will stay as he is.
If you treat him as if he were what he ought to be
and could be, he will become the bigger and better man.
—Goethe

J don't understand why he does the things he does!"
Ever said that to yourself?

Do you ever wonder about some of the following?

- *Why*, when you and your husband go shopping together (and by together, yes, we mean that once-a-decade experience) does he know so precisely what he wants, enter the store, buy it on the spot, and then want to go home?

To a man, shopping is like a hunt. He knows his target, sights it, shoots it, bags it, and drags it home. His focused, compartmentalized brain doesn't get distracted from his goal. Shopping to him is not an experience but rather a way of accomplishing something, a goal to conquer. Now that he's "dragged it home," he wants to move onto his next target.

- *Why*, when you play a game or sport together, is he always so competitive, or, if you forget to keep score, he can get so upset?

Competition is the name of the game in a man's world. So is winning, proving himself, and "pressing the envelope." The world to him is one to be challenged and tested. A man reasons, "Why would you play a game if you aren't trying to win? And if you play and don't keep score, that's a waste of time, because nobody will know who won!"

- *Why* doesn't he seem to pick up your cues when you're upset, even though you give him plenty of sighs or "the look"? Or why does he always have to ask, "What's the matter?" You figure he should just know.

Men don't pick up cues, clues, sighs, or looks like women do. A man's brain isn't wired to pick up the subtleties you give off with your body language. He's in another compartment when you're doing that. Ladies, he's clueless as to what you want unless you *tell* him. And that last sentence is a "hot tip" for you, for this is one major factor that is an irritant to men: They don't like having to *guess* what you want, for they assume they'll always be wrong in their guessing. He figures, "Why play the game if I know I'm going to lose?"

- *Why*, when he's on the road and lost, won't he stop and ask for directions?

Asking for help is an admission of weakness, a lack of competence. Men can't have that hanging over them. Men are always proving to themselves and others that they can perform competently. That's one of the reasons a man always may be pushing himself to success—to excel—to win.

- *Why*, when you have a conversation with your husband, doesn't he seem to remember much of it two hours later?

True, often he just isn't listening, but a major part of it is because of our sex differences and the way our memories work. Women can store more random and irrelevant information than a man can. Most men can do this only if the information is organized into some coherent form. If in a conversation between a husband and wife they bounce from one topic to another and loop around back again, he probably won't remember most of it because it's not *organized* for his memory.

Men also tend to remember things only if they have specific relevance to him. Knowing about the mail carrier's children may not seem relevant to his life.

Yes, We Are "Very" Different

Yes, your husband is *very* different from you. Those differences range from personality differences to background differences, but they're mainly because he's a male and you're a female.

Isn't it amazing that males and females come from the same Homo sapiens species, but our similarities are worlds apart? Recent years have seen an explosion of studies on the workings of the male and female brains. Scientists have discovered that many differences between the two sexes that were once credited to social conditioning are really biological in nature. They have found that the interplay of hormones on brains that are prewired male and prewired female is what actually makes for the differences.[1]

Why do we say all this? Because you need to realize that men aren't strange or weird (well, maybe a few are), but that they're simply very different from women. And with these differences they have needs different from a woman. In this chapter we'll see another demonstration of God's desire to meet our needs. We'll see the interplay between a husband's needs and a wife's role in the marriage demonstrated by God in the Bible.

Your husband's greatest emotional need is for *significance*. He wants to know that who he is and what he does is important and makes a difference. God created him as a doer and a conqueror—to have dominion over his territory and to subdue the earth (Gen. 1:26, 28). That's why he's always pushing himself to prove that he's a can-do man. Little boys are an example of that when at a certain point in their young lives they will say to their parents, "No, let me do it. I can do it." They want to prove themselves to others and themselves.

A man derives much of his identity through his work. It's a way of demonstrating to himself and to the world that he matters by what he does. The downside to this is that his focused drive to succeed at work can become so compelling that he can end up neglecting his wife and children. But work is important to who he is. This explains why most men become so devastated if they lose their jobs. It's as if he has lost a piece of the puzzle of his life that makes him who he is. He's also devastated if he believes you don't think what he does is important or that you even resent his work. He equates that with how you really feel about him as a husband.

In his world a man fears failure. Failure is not an option for him even to consider. Anything that makes him feel incompetent is a threat to him and something he will retreat from—such as a wife who makes him feel he cannot accomplish something. He needs to believe he can succeed.

When Bob Jr. attended Florida State University, he had many talks with us about two young ladies he liked. We asked him which one of the two made him feel significant. His fast response was "Misti." A few weeks later Misti was his one and only girlfriend, and a couple of years later Bob Sr. had the honor of officiating at the wedding of Bob Jr. to Misti.

Yvonne Will Take It from Here

Yvonne will write the rest of this chapter for women, for the same reason that Bob wrote a large portion of the previous chapter for men.

Even though I teach husbands how to love their wives, they're always wanting me to make sure the wives understand that certain areas are important to them, so that they can live out their role as husbands.

When we women understand what drives and motivates a man, we start to better understand why he does the things he does. Hopefully, with that knowledge added to what the Bible says about a wife's role in marriage, we then have a solid way to go about meeting his needs.

When I finally understood what men need, I realized that so many ways I was dealing with Bob had caused him to feel he was incompetent. No wonder he often retreated from me. I had to learn a new way to interact with my husband. It was not always easy, but the Lord gave me the strength and courage to carry through. I now see benefits of learning what my role is in our marriage and fulfilling it in the way that will meet Bob's needs. What a major difference this made in our relationship! Instead of a husband who retreats, I have a husband who draws close to me. We are truly *teammates*.

The Wife's Role

Let's begin with what the Bible says a wife's role is to be. In Gen. 2:18 God said, "It is not good for the man to be alone. I will make a helper suitable for him." This was originally written in Hebrew; the Hebrew word for "helper" means *complement*. The wife's role is to be a helper—a complement—to her husband.

Unfortunately, too many women read that verse and see it this way: "My job as a wife is to remake my husband."

It's amazing how a woman looks at her husband-to-be before she marries him. He is her knight in shining armor who is, if not perfect, close to it. He sweeps her away as they ride his horse to his castle, and the happy couple will live happily ever after. The only problem is that after "the two become one," they start fighting about *which* one. Then as she takes a closer look at her knight, she starts to see all the rust spots on his armor and so figures she'll just take her rust remover and remove a spot here, a spot there. By doing this she thinks he will be so much better off.

God does not instruct the wife to remake her husband, but rather to *complete* him. Remember: The word "helper" means a complement suitable for him. Wives are to help their husbands in areas in which they're lacking. A wife is to balance her husband. A husband cannot do without his wife. Oh, yes—he can *exist* with out her, but he can't truly live the life that God wants for him if she is not his teammate. A wife is the only person who can look in the dresser drawer and find her husband's socks after he says, "My socks must not be there—I can't find them."

Too often when women hear the word "helper," they get a picture of someone less important than, or secondary to, the man—that by being a helper we are just waiting for him to tell us what to do. This is certainly not what the word means in scripture.

In the Old Testament the word "helper" was used to refer to God as our Helper (Ps. 33:20). In the New Testament Jesus is described as our Helper (Heb. 4:16), as is the Holy Spirit (Rom. 8:26). We wouldn't think of the Trinity as being secondary to us because they are our Helpers. Rather, the roles the Trinity fulfills benefit each of us. Being called a helper is a high calling. It is a mighty role. Do you look at it that way?

Coming Alongside Him

To be a helpmate means you come alongside of your mate. Your husband can't succeed nearly as well without you. He needs your help to become what God intends for him to be. Have you heard the saying "Behind every great man is a surprised mother-in-law?" A more accurate one is "Behind every great man is his wife."

There's a story about a husband and wife taking a walk together. The husband was the chief executive officer of his business. As they strolled together the husband said, "Look—there's your old high school sweetheart. I hear he's still hauling fertilizer for a living. Just think—if you had married that guy, you'd be the wife of a fertilizer hauler."

The wife replied, "No, if I had married him, he would be the president of that company."

We are important to our husbands. Here's what the Bible says about a good wife: "If you can find a truly good wife, she is worth more than precious gems! Her husband can trust her, and she will richly satisfy his needs. She will not hinder him, but help him all her life" (Prov. 31:10-12, TLB).

The role of a wife revolves around helping and loving her husband and children. A major obstacle these days is the many tempting options available for women. When a woman subjects herself to too many of them, she becomes stressed and eventually has little or no energy or time to give support to her husband. If she doesn't fulfill her role, her home can become unstable.

This is an area a husband and wife need to revisit frequently—to make sure nothing is preventing her from fulfilling her role. Bob and I did this just a while back. With no children at home, I had become busier in our ministry, traveling and speaking. But I found myself so busy with work that Bob's needs were always getting shuttled to the end of the line. Fortunately, I have a husband who doesn't complain, but I became aware that this wasn't going to be a short-term situation. It was possibly heading toward being permanent unless I did something about it. I told Bob that I felt uncomfortable about the fact that he was always getting the short end of the stick. We talked and prayed about some alternatives. We mutually decided I needed to be relieved of some work responsibilities so my focus could be on him and our speaking, in that order. As I walked away, I heard him let out a big "Hallelujah!"

The Four Cs

Just as with the husbands, let's get practical about how we as wives can live out our role as helpers. I call them "the four Cs." Sounds like a 1960s singing group, doesn't it? In this case "the four Cs" are four ways to meet your mate's need for significance.

As you read these things your husband needs from you, you may say, "Wait a minute. *I* need these too!" Understood, but please remember—we already wrote about *your* needs in the last chapter. Now it's his turn. I want you to focus on what you need to give to your husband. God will use that in a way to meet your needs as well.

"C" No. 1—Be His Cheerleader

Your husband needs your approval of who he is and what he does. It's part of being a male. Little boys playing in their backyards will always yell, "Mom, Dad—look at me! Look at what I can do!" They're showing off, strutting their stuff.

As they get older, teenage boys will do things like belly flopping off a diving board into a swimming pool, hoping the girls are watching, wanting their attention and approval. Many go out for sports and hope the girls will look at what they can do and think, "He's the greatest."

Our husbands are the same, also looking for approval when they do things. If a man isn't getting the appreciation at home, he might go to a neighbor's house and fix something. It might even be the same thing you want fixed in your house. Why the neighbor's house and not yours? Maybe it's because the neighbor makes such comments as "That's a terrific job" or "Wow— you're really good at what you do!" In contrast, at home he hears only "You didn't do it right." As his wife, think about that.

Your husband can't hear praises enough. When he receives constant praises from you, just picture him with his chest raised up and thinking, "Yes, I can conquer the world." Plus, no husband ever told his wife she talks too much when she's telling him how wonderful he is.

Be Careful of Complaints and Criticism

Believe it or not, your husband's goal is to make you happy. He wants to please you.

Thirty-five-year-old Jonathan told me during one of the men-only sessions I conducted. "I've always wanted to do the special little things for my wife that you speak about, but I never seem to please her. Two years ago I planned a special romantic weekend at a nice resort for us. I took care of all the details, even getting the baby-sitter, as well as having roses in the room when we arrived. Do you think she was happy? No. All I got all weekend was complaints, such as 'You shouldn't have spent so much money on this' and 'The food in the restaurant wasn't that great.' She told me she would have been just as happy staying home with me for the weekend. Yeah, right. We do that and she complains that I never take her anywhere. I've given up trying to please her, because I can't do anything right. I wish just once—*just once*—she would appreciate something I've done for her." There was sadness in that man's eyes.

That's one man's story, but he's indicative of thousands I interact with yearly with the same or similar stories. A husband will give up on his relationship because he feels powerless in trying to fulfill her. Husbands figure, "Why set myself up for more failure? It's easier to just avoid it."

Jonathan's story became all the more interesting to me because right after he made his remarks to me and excused himself, his wife approached me and started complaining: "My husband never does anything special for me." Strange—she was sabotaging her own happiness through her complaints and criticism but never connected it to her husband's lack of desire to do anything special for her.

As a wife, don't be like the woman spoken about in Prov. 21:19. "Better to live in a desert than with a quarrelsome and ill-tempered wife." Moral: Do *not* complain when he does something special for you. Why? Criticism is hard enough to take from anyone else but is especially difficult coming from your spouse. In your husband's case, it strikes at the very core of who he is and at his competence. Hurtful criticism doesn't motivate him to right behavior. It only causes him to want to give up. Trust me—I know from personal experience. Always keep in mind that it's through his actions that he often connects with his feelings. When you show appreciation for his actions, he feels loved.

As women, we fall into the trap of complaining so easily. Prov. 19:13 tells us what we sound like to our husbands: "A nagging wife annoys like constant dripping" (TLB). To him we're like that annoying faucet that drips, drips, drips when you're trying to fall asleep. Ugh! We have to be careful.

One couple who constantly bickered over everything decided to call a truce and stop arguing for one week. Each time they got upset and wanted to express it orally, they agreed to write it down instead. Whatever she wrote down she would put into the "his" box, and he would put his jottings into the "her" box. At the end of the week they were to go through their boxes. Saturday arrived, and he pulled out "his" box and found notes saying, "You never pick up your clothes, and I'm tired of being your maid," "You've been promising to mow the yard for 10 days now and it's still not done," plus many, many more. He felt bad that he had offended her so often. Now it was her turn. She opened up the first paper and read it, then the next one, the next one, and so on until she read them all. Tears welled up in her eyes. They all said, "I love you very much."

You may be asking, "Does she mean I shouldn't say anything negative about what he does?" No, that's not what I mean. The factor here is the *timing*. Remember the famous saying from *Mary Poppins:* "A spoonful of sugar helps the medicine go down." Correct timing can be like the sugar.

I remember how timing affected a situation dealing with our laundry. Bob helps me with many household duties. One of them is the laundry. One day I put a load in the washing machine and asked him to finish the process, since I was going to be gone for several hours. He said, "Sure." When I got home, I discovered he had put something into the dryer that never should have gone there, and it shrunk. My immediate reaction was to find him and criticize him for what he had done.

But it was as if the Lord placed a large flashing stop sign in front of me with the words "Reconsider your actions" printed boldly on it. I went to Bob and thanked him for his help and let him know I appreciated it. If I had looked like a Rambo-ette charging down the hall, ready to fire my criticism bazooka at him, you can be sure he wouldn't be so agreeable to help with the laundry the next time. Why? Because he would figure, "Why bother, since evidently I can't do it right or do it to please her?" Then I would be back to doing the laundry all by myself.

I waited two days before I brought up the subject about that item that shouldn't have gone into the dryer and explained why. He listened and was receptive to watch it the next time. This way I still had what every wife wants—a laundry partner!

Ask yourself this question: "Where is my focus?" On all the things he has done wrong, or on all the things he has done right, do you give him more criticism or more praise?

Two Choices

In learning to be Bob's cheerleader, I found that the way I phrase something makes a difference. Once when Bob was leaving for a weekend at a men's conference, he told me he would call when he arrived. Knowing he would get to the retreat center at 5 P.M., I assumed he would call me around 7:00. That would give him a couple of hours to settle in. Keep in mind that we never talked about a particular time, just that he would call when he arrived. I waited and waited and didn't get the call until 9:30.

I had two choices when I heard his voice. One choice was to complain, "How come you didn't call me earlier? I've been waiting and waiting for your call!" Frankly I was a bit tempted, but I also knew that if I spoke that way I would have made him feel that he had done something wrong. Do you think he would have been pleased to talk with me? I don't think so.

The other choice was to say, "Hi, Honey. I'm so glad you got there safely and that you called. I've been looking forward to hearing your wonderful voice." Words like that, which would give him an incentive to call me again. Fortunately, I chose the second of the two, and he called me several more times that weekend.

Gratitude Notes

I've found another way that has helped me change my focus on the things my husband does right: I write him "gratitude notes." I'm a very verbal person, and so I frequently speak compliments to Bob. Those are important, of course, but I had nearly forgotten the power of the written word. So I started writing "gratitude notes" to Bob nearly every day—such as "Thank You, Lord, for my husband, who isn't too proud to apologize. I'm grateful for him." Or "Thank You, Lord, for giving me a husband who is so generous, especially when it comes to sharing his popcorn." It's seeing the little everyday things in life and letting him know that you appreciate him, not taking your husband for granted. It certainly has changed my attitude about my husband, because I'm now more focused on his good points.

But here's the kicker. I knew Bob liked the notes I left for him to read at various places around our house, but I didn't realize how much until one speaking trip we were on. I had to go into his briefcase for a file. As I was rummaging around, I found a bunch of the notes I had written him. Since I was curious about why he carried them with him, I asked.

Bob: *I told her that not only did I enjoy reading them, but I was blessed to reread them. When I do, it always gives me a lift when I realize how much my wife appreciates who I am and what I do.*

A small gesture? Yes, but a powerful one. Be his cheerleader.

"C" No. 2—Be His Champion

You are a mirror to your husband. You reflect back to him strong messages about who he is, his manhood, and his masculinity in his marriage to you. That's why scripture says to respect your husband (Eph. 5:33).

He so strongly desires to know that his wife thinks he's important, that who he is and what he does is of value. It builds his confidence and desire to live up to his role as a husband. If he feels worthwhile, he loves himself, and then he'll love you. And when he loves you he then wants to lead you. If he doesn't receive a strong, loving, encouraging message from his wife, he'll have a continual sense of frustration.

Halfway through speaking at a Midwest pastors-and-spouses' conference, a pastor told us he felt he was a broken man, suffering in his marriage and family. He felt broken, he said, because his wife didn't show the respect to him that he deeply desired. We could see as we observed her that she showed a definite *lack* of respect with her attitude and actions

toward him. He told us he had lost all confidence in his work as
a pastor and as a husband.

We need to be our mate's encouragement coach. We need
to be the main person in his life to spur him on to be a stronger
husband, father, and Christian man. That's what Heb. 10:24-25
speaks about: "Consider how we may spur one another on toward love and good deeds. . . . let us encourage one another."

You have a choice when dealing with your husband—to
champion him or crush him, because you know best his vulnerable areas, his weaknesses. But you also know his areas of
strength and greatest potential. God has given you the choice
of which way to go and what type of wife you will be. Prov.
14:1 says, "The wise woman builds her house, but with her
own hands the foolish one tears hers down." Let's contrast the
two.

A Foolish Woman Versus a Wise Woman

- A foolish woman will be sarcastic about something her
  husband is going to do, saying something like "Now
  don't blow it like you usually do." That's a put-down.
  Your attitude will affect your action. If you think he can't
  do anything (which isn't true), then your attitude will
  come across in what you say and how you say it. A wise
  woman will give encouraging words like "I know you'll
  do a good job."

- A foolish woman will interrupt her husband's conversation in a group when he's speaking and start a conversation with another person right in the middle of his talking. The message she is giving him and the others is that
  she doesn't think what he has to say is important, or
  she's bored with what he's saying. A wise woman will
  look at her husband and listen while he speaks. Even if
  she's heard the same story 22 times, she will wait until
  he's finished before speaking.

- A foolish woman will tell her mother, sister, and close
  friends all of her husband's faults when she's upset with
  him. That humiliates him. That's gossip. And she's be-
  traying him. A wise woman will be careful what she
  shares, especially in public, and will never intentionally
  slander her husband. Remember: When everything is

patched up between the husband and wife, the ones she tattled to will still be thinking ill of him.

- A foolish woman will ridicule, correct, or challenge her husband in public. This deeply embarrasses him and cuts him to the very core of who he is. It can build deep resentment inside him. A wise woman will keep her lips zipped. If there is an area that needs correction, she will deal with it in private, and only with her husband. She will make positive statements about him in public, just as he should be doing for her.

- A foolish woman argues or corrects her husband when he's dealing with the children, and to worsen the matter, does it in front of the children. Or she will put him down to the children. A wise woman will discuss the kids with him in private and never belittle him in front of the children.

- A foolish woman will compare her husband with other men, making such statements as "My father didn't do that. He used to . . ." or "Christine's husband does it [this way or that way]." A wise woman realizes that such comparisons aren't fair, because she shouldn't compare her husband's weaknesses with another man's strength. Instead, she'll focus on his strengths and gifts and tell him about them often.

I can't stress this too many times: *don't live like the foolish woman.* I speak from two different perspectives. After I've spoken to husbands about loving their wives, those in deep pain will come up and ask what to do because their wives don't respect them or appreciate the things they do. My heart aches when I talk to so many hurting, broken men. But I also understand this from a personal perspective.

For years I lived as the foolish woman. I wasn't giving Bob what he needed. It hurts me to even mention it now, but I can't change history. That's the bad news. The good news is that our relationship has changed tremendously since those years. As teammates we have prayed over and discussed these matters, forgiven each other, and moved on. But it took me many years to repair the damage I had done. My counsel to you is simply this: Why waste that precious commodity known as time if you can do it right the first time?

That Dreaded "S" Word

If I would say, "Men, name three happy words that begin with 's,'" do you know what they would say? "Sports," "steak," and "sex." If I asked the same question to a group of women, they might reply with, "Shopping, shopping, and shopping."

If I would say, "Men, name any unhappy words that begin with 's,'" they might be hard-pressed to think of any. But if I were to say, "Ladies, what dreaded word comes to your mind that starts with 's,'" the word "submission" might easily come up.

That's right. To many women, "submission" is a dreaded word. Yet a way to be your husband's champion and show respect is through the response of submission. Eph. 5:22 says, "Wives, *submit* to your husbands as to the Lord" (emphasis added).

Whenever we bring up the "s" word in our seminars, we often see two different responses, depending on the gender of the person. The men seem to sit up a bit straighter in their chairs, become attentive, and give each other high fives.

Many women, however, seem to stiffen and grit their teeth. Is that how you're feeling right now? Does that word conjure up thoughts of your being a doormat that your husband will walk all over? Or never being able to fully express your own opinions unless you receive his royal permission, because hubby will be making all the decisions and will tell you what to do? Do you picture a power relationship? Sadly, this is what is being played out in many homes across this country, but this is *not* what the Bible teaches concerning submission.

To understand submission, we as wives need to look to Jesus for our example, just as our husbands look to Him for their role as a servant leader. Our submission is compared to the Church's submission to Christ, as in Eph. 5:22-24: "Wives, submit to your husbands as to the Lord. For the husband is the head of the wife as Christ is the head of the church, his body, of which he is the Savior. Now as the church submits to Christ, so also wives should submit to their husbands in everything."

Such submission is not negative, but positive and freeing. It can be that way for us wives. And to be in submission doesn't place you in a lower role—not at all. Remember that Jesus is equal to the Father (John 10:30), but Jesus submits to the Father's authority over Him (1 Cor. 15:28).

Submission is a response to the husband's leadership that empowers him to love and lead you as Christ does His Church. But if a wife resists his attempts to lead and even competes with him for leadership, he will at first resist, and then he will retreat. He figures that if he can't succeed at home because of the constant resistance he's receiving, he'll just give up and focus his time and energy on leading at his job. This will leave a gaping void in his family, but instead of giving out to his wife to meet her needs, he'll go inward and focus on himself and his needs.

For years I struggled with this whole idea of submission, mainly because I didn't understand the biblical view of what it is supposed to be. I fought Bob about his leadership each step of the way. I would verbally refuse to follow. I would manipulate him to get him to do things my way, and we women can be professionals in the manipulation game. I now reflect on what I used to do and am ashamed of how I didn't show a loving attitude toward my husband.

Bob fought me for the leadership position for years but eventually threw in the towel. I'm surprised he hung in there as long as he did, especially with all the resistance I was giving him. After he retreated and buried himself in his work, I complained that he should take over the leadership role again. Would you, with a wife like me? I doubt it. Knowing what I know now, neither would I. After a while, I reasoned that since he wasn't leading, I should go ahead as I had been. Our whole relationship got turned upside down. That's the bad news.

The good news is that when God started putting our relationship back together and teaching us about how to live as teammates with our different but equally important roles, our marriage started to grow.

Often a wife may think she's being submissive because of her actions, but it's her *attitude* that comes across as one of possible noncompliance.

It's like a little boy riding with his father in a convertible who keeps standing up in the front seat. His dad tells him twice to sit down and buckle up, but the boy keeps unbuckling and standing up again. Finally the father says, "Listen—either sit down, buckle up, and stay there, or I'll pull this car over and we'll just wait until you do." So the boy sits down, buckles up, folds his arms, and says, "My bottom is sitting down, but on the inside I'm still standing up."

The little boy demonstrates an outward behavior of submission, but his inward attitude is one of a rebellious spirit. That's *not* what God meant when He spoke of submission.

An Attitude of Love That Desires to Cooperate

One definition of "submission" is "an attitude of love that desires to cooperate." Did you get that? Reread it. It's first an attitude; then it goes forth into action. It springs from the heart. It's a release within our spirit so we will encourage our husbands in their leadership role, as opposed to fighting them every step of the way.

Are you aware that it's through your submission that God can direct your husband? 1 Pet. 3:1 directs, "Wives, in the same way be submissive to your husbands so that, if any of them do not believe the word, they may be won over without words by the behavior of their wives." This is for unbelieving husbands as well as believers who are in disobedience or are not growing.

Often what stops us from submitting to our husbands is the fear that they will not take our best interests in mind. 1 John 4:18 says, "Perfect love drives out fear." If you love someone and he or she loves you, you will not be afraid to submit. I discovered that my fear wasn't always directed toward my husband but toward the Lord. I realized I didn't believe He truly cared about all the details of my life and that He would work out what would be best for me. I had to reread, believe, and claim Prov. 3:5-6: "Trust in the LORD with all your heart and lean not on your own understanding; in all your ways acknowledge him, and he will make your paths straight."

We must keep those verses in our minds and hearts in those times, even when we can see what will probably happen and can sense it probably won't work. We must walk by faith, not by sight (2 Cor. 5:7).

At this point you have a choice as a wife. You can push to have your way and do it through manipulation, which can include pouting, whining, tears, or an overabundance of nonstop words. If you do that, then you're telling God to get out of your way because you can handle this matter much better than He can. Go ahead and do this if you want more strife in your marriage.

Or—you can release it all into God's loving, caring hands so He can work it out according to His will and in His timing. He will work in your situations by either changing your husband as He speaks to his heart, or helping you *grow* through it as you *go* through it (Rom. 8:38). Do you believe God can take care of any situation you're in? That's right—He can and He will.

"I Told You So"

Right now you might be thinking, "What if I submit and he makes a mistake?" Be real. We *all* make mistakes. He does. You do. We all do, so please don't point a holier-than-thou finger and say something like "I told you so. If you had only listened to me." In place of that classic downer of words, extend grace. You would like grace extended to you if the positions were reversed. This will allow your husband to regroup, and quite possibly he'll reflect on how positively you handled this situation when something like this comes up again.

I've written about how submission empowers your husband to lead, but here's a word of caution: neither Bob nor I believe a wife is to submit to a husband's illegal, immoral, sinful behavior. I spoke privately to a woman after one of our marriage seminars who related to me a sad story about her marriage. She said, "About 10 years ago my husband started looking at pornographic magazines. Of course, this bothered me, to have my husband looking at the bodies of other females. I would tell him how much it bothered me and that I didn't think that was a right thing to do to me, to himself, and before God. He would always counter that it was his decision to do that and that I had to submit to his decision.

"Eventually the magazines gave way to pornographic videos, which became a regular diet. He then wanted to do sexually with me what he was watching on those videos, and said that if I didn't go along with his wishes, he would either force me to do them, as I had to submit to his will, or he would knock me around."

This lady wanted to know if being a submissive wife meant she was to go along with what her husband desired in this area. Without hesitation I told her that abuse by a husband should never be tolerated or submitted to and that submission is for empowering a husband to do what God desires for him to do. It is *not* for enabling a husband to carry out wrong, sinful behavior. I told her that both of them needed to seek professional counseling, preferably together, and that she should not be silent about this situation.

A husband needs to know that he *cannot demand* that his wife submit to him. God has told him to love her and lead her in the way Christ does the Church. Out of that comes her response to her husband.

"C" No. 3—Be His Companion

Picture Adam in the Garden of Eden prior to Eve's appearance. Adam realized he was lonely right in the midst of naming all the animals. The picture became a little brighter when God provided for his loneliness by creating Eve to be his companion. 1 Cor. 11:9 says, "Neither was man created for woman, but woman for man."

Bob has often told me that he more fully understands that verse when I'm in Washington visiting my family for a week to 10 days. Because of our companionship with each other and our growing closeness to our Lord, he has told me, "When you're gone from me, it's as though part of me is missing. As each day passes by, I become lonelier without you. You're my companion. I feel incomplete when you're away from me, so I really look forward to the day you return to me." You can well imagine what those words do to my heart.

Being his companion is being his friend. We both believe that you and your mate can be *best* friends. There are three ways you can be that friend.

1. Be His Companion by Being Interested in the Things He's Interested In

For many couples, during their dating and in the first years of marriage, they shared many of the man's interests. But after some time the two of them began to go their separate ways. Often the wife would think, "For my husband it's probably no big deal that we're not involved together with his interest." But it *is* a big deal. One of the reasons a man marries a woman is to have a companion to share the things that interest him.

Bob likes football—*really* likes it. He enjoys every level of it, whether it's peewee football, high school, college, or pro. He hopes there will be a Super Bowl game in heaven every 24 hours. For many years he coached football both on the high school and collegiate levels. It's a part of him. Before we were married I would attend games with him, watch the games on television, and listen as he talked football with me. Within a couple of years of our marriage I started finding excuses for not attending or watching the games. The excuses came more frequently. At first Bob didn't show his disappointment, but after a while he stopped talking football with me. For a long time I didn't realize how important it was to share this interest with him.

Willard Harley points out in his book *His Needs, Her Needs* that "spending recreational time with his wife is second only to sex for the typical husband."[2] Ladies, you know how important sex is to him, and this runs a close second. Yes, it *is* important.

When I more fully understood the importance of the two of us sharing some of his interests, I made a change. I became interested in his interests, like football. Now understand that Bob is no longer coaching, and he doesn't watch that many football games anymore because of his focused priority on ministry. But take for example when he's in his den doing some work and he has a game on television. When a great play occurs, he calls me into the room so he can have me watch the replay with him. He likes explaining both the artistry and science of the play to me, and as the years go by I now more readily understand certain plays and can appreciate the skills involved. We share this.

Another area of interest for my husband is working out at the gym. This has been a part of his life since his late teens. Even though I was knowledgeable in nutrition, exercise was never my thing. (How many women can relate to that statement?) Over the past 18 years I've joined him at the gym. I now enjoy working out because it gives me so many benefits—like stabilizing my weight, sleeping better, and reducing stress. But the best benefit is that I'm sharing something with my husband that's important to him. I like to tease him and say, "Honey, the only reason you want me at the gym with you is that you know I'm your biggest fan, so that when you show off for me by lifting those heavy weights, I can 'Ooo' and 'Ah' for you."

(**Bob:** *If she only knew that as the years have gone by I'm somewhat weaker than when I was younger, so I'm now pumpin' tinfoil, no longer pumpin' iron!*)

2. Be His Companion by Sharing His Dreams

There will be days or even weeks when your husband may become discouraged at work and wonder if he should be doing something else. There may be a time or two in your marriage when he'll be asking himself, "Does my life really stand for anything?" He'll start to dream—"I wonder what life would be like if I could . . . ?" Those are the times he'll want to share his dreams and ideas with you, because you're his teammate for life. He needs to have the confidence of knowing that you'll not overreact or respond in a negative manner to his ideas. Remember—he's being vulnerable by sharing these with you. The challenge to you comes from some of his ideas that may sound a bit strange or off-the-wall to you.

Jim and Cindy live in a suburb of a major city here in California that features all the amenities of city life at their fingertips. When Jim started dreaming about selling everything, packing up, moving to Alaska, building a log cabin, and living off the land, she freaked out. She could not picture herself cooking over a woodstove, washing clothes in a bucket, using an outhouse, and always wondering if a bear or wolf would drop by unannounced for lunch—and she would be the lunch! She told me, "I've learned in 20 years of marriage to let Jim dream instead of telling him all the reasons his dreams would never work. I used to do this, and he stopped dreaming with me. Now I listen and ask questions and pray. To be honest with you, depending on what he brings up, sometimes I do a whole lot of praying! It worked with the Alaska dream. We didn't move there, but we did go on an Alaskan cruise. That was enough for him."

Cindy's attitude was under the Holy Spirit's control, especially as she laughed during the last part of her statement.

I used to come unglued when Bob shared some of his dreams with me, because I felt it would rock my security. I know now that my security is in the Lord. The Lord wants the best for my life and will take care of me. That's His promise, and I truly believe Him. Knowing this has given me the confidence to say to Bob when he presents his ideas and dreams, "Honey, I'll follow you anywhere because I know you and the Lord will always take good care of me." It has been interesting to note that some of my husband's dreams have stayed just that—dreams. There have been others that have come to fruition and have been great for our family. Let your husband dream with you.

3. Be His Companion by Letting Him Know He's Needed

I clearly remember my father saying to me when I was in my late teens, "Even though you're quite capable of doing many things, don't do everything. Otherwise when you marry, your husband will never feel needed." I only wish I had heeded my father's wise advice earlier than I did. I figured that if I could do something, why have Bob do it?

For example, when he would begin carrying in the groceries from the car, I would say to him, "I can bring them in." Eventually he stopped asking if he could help me, because I always declined his offer. It was the same with many other things. After a while he started feeling I didn't need him for much.

What got my attention to make a change was watching the relationship between a neighbor husband and wife. There were many little things he would do for her, and I thought, "How sweet! I wonder why Bob doesn't do things like that for me." Then it dawned on me that I had been telling him for years not to bother. Guess what? He *didn't* bother. I had created this situation myself. The point wasn't whether I could or could not carry in the groceries. Physically, of course, I could, but more important, I recognized that I had taken away my husband's joy in wanting to serve me because I made him feel he wasn't needed.

Don't Compete with Him

This illustration brings up another point: Don't compete with your husband or try to show him up, as if he isn't up to speed in many areas of life like you are. For instance, don't compete with his Christianity.

A man named Kyle told me, "I learned early on that I couldn't measure up to my wife when it came to spiritual matters. I always felt inadequate around her. Whenever we had a conversation, she would always quote scripture to me about everything I said. She would place the Bible and books all over the house and have them opened to key spots she wanted me to read. She had Scripture verses taped to everything I owned, even my electric drill. Now in themselves there was nothing 'wrong' with that, but I constantly felt she was jamming her spiritual superiority in my face. I know my responding actions weren't right, but I started retreating and virtually stopped growing in my faith; then I stopped going to church. I just wish she would have encouraged me rather than discouraged me in my spiritual walk."

"C" No. 4—Be His Complement

Being your husband's complement is helping him become the man God desires him to be. Keep in mind that though you are his complement, you are not his preacher. Too often a woman falls into the trap of playing the role of Holy Spirit in her husband's life. She feels she knows what areas he needs to change in, so she figures she can just help God out a bit. He's a very busy God and would probably appreciate some help. Yeah, right!

A wife can also think she's the natural one for the job, because who could love her husband more than she does? What we wives need to realize is that God loves our husbands *much more* than we do, and it's His desire for our husbands to grow as part of His pure, holy motives. Ours can often be selfish. Don't assume God's responsibility.

This doesn't mean that God won't use us to cause a change. What it does mean is that we need to get out of God's way and let Him be the one to make that determination. When there's an area in your husband that you feel needs to be addressed, go to God *first* with your request *before* you go to your husband.

The reason we do this is to remind us that God will supply all of our needs in the way that will be perfect for both of us. Far too often we don't consult God first, and we run off to our husbands and try to fix everything. That usually leads to frustration.

"Frustrated" described a woman who came up to us at a couples' retreat and complained, "My husband isn't fulfilling his role of leading and loving me. I leave books on a man's role all over the house, with the pages wide open. I've even underlined the key paragraphs on those open pages. I've placed them in the bathroom, in his den, on the bed, everywhere. I've bought tapes on marriage and put them in the car so that when he turns on the cassette during his commute he will automatically hear them. I'm constantly urging him to go to seminars or the men's group, but he just doesn't seem interested. He doesn't seem to appreciate any of my help, and he refuses to make any changes in his life. What else can I do?"

I took a deep breath and jumped in by saying, "Stop doing all those things. Frankly, get off his back. Start praying for your husband, and start praying for your own attitude. Ask the Holy Spirit to do His work in him. You are making him feel that he could never measure up to what you want, so he feels the easiest way to deal with this is to shut you out.

She wasn't very happy with my comment, because what she really wanted was three easy steps to get her husband to do what she wanted. But it isn't about getting our husbands to do what we want. It's about creating an environment in our marriages so our husbands can hear what God wants for them and then encouraging them as they step out to do it. It's about creating an environment in our marriages that can motivate our mates to change.

Inner Conviction Is Stronger than Outer Stimulation

I have found that inner conviction is stronger than outer stimulation when it comes to making a change. What I mean is that when I get out of the way and let God show Bob areas in his life that need changing, the changes are solid.

When something surfaces that I feel needs to be addressed with Bob, I first pray and ask God for my game plan. Sometimes I feel such a reservation about saying anything that I just keep quiet, pray, and watch God do the work in my husband. At other times I may get a strong prompting from the Holy Spirit to go to Bob about a certain area. But I make sure it's a clear signal from the Lord and not just my own desires and emotions sending me on the way.

I remember the first time I exercised this option. I prayed and did not feel a release to go talk to Bob, so I kept praying. In a matter of days Bob came to me and told me the Lord had been working on him in an area he felt he needed to make a change. It was the same area about which I was concerned and praying. After he spoke to me, I thought, "Hey—this works!"

A week later I tried it a second time. Same results as the first time. Then I thought, "Hey—this is easy. Just tell God what I want changed, and it will be changed quickly." So I tried it the third time, but I didn't get the same results. In fact, this particular area went on for months with no change. It took over a year for anything to happen, but when it did occur—although the timing was different than I wanted—I could see where the timing was just right, because God was in control. Plus—it turned out a bit differently than I originally anticipated, but that too showed to be just right and even better than I initially requested. God *was* definitely in control.

God had me realize that He isn't a magic genie who does what I want on my command but that when I bring my requests to Him, He'll do what's best in every situation (Phil. 4:6). I have often found that it's really me whom God is working on in a certain situation, and many times He's teaching me to change my expectations or my response to Bob. That's what Paul meant in Phil. 4:19 when he wrote, "My God will meet all your needs according to his glorious riches in Christ Jesus."

Team-Building Questions

1. Is your first aim in your marriage to be your mate's helper? If not, why not?
2. When you think of the word "helper," what words come to mind? Read Ps. 33:20; Heb. 4:16; and Rom. 8:26. Is your view correct as to how the word "helper" is used in the Scriptures?
3. Are you the foolish woman or the wise woman listed in Prov. 14:1? If foolish, what changes can you make in your life?
4. When you communicate with your mate, do you do it in a way that shows respect, or disrespect?
5. Do you have a problem with submission? Read Rom. 13:1-2; Eph. 5:21; 1 Pet. 3:1-6; Prov. 3:5-6; 2 Cor. 5:7; and Rom. 8:28. Ask the Lord to give you insight into each verse as you read it.

Team-Building Action Steps

1. List one practical thing you can do to meet your husband's need for a

   cheerleader_____

   champion _____

   companion _____

   complement _____

2. Ask your mate to participate with you on this one. Separately, each of you make a list of all the things you both like to do together. Come together, exchange lists, and rank each other's list as to which would bring you the most enjoyment. From that rank, come up with a list of things you both would like to do together. Decide how much time you will spend doing the activities together.

3. Consider writing your husband gratitude notes. Do it for two weeks and see what the results are.

Father, thank You for creating me
as a complement suitable for my husband.
Help me view him not as a makeover job
but as one who deserves my acceptance,
respect, and admiration. In Jesus' name. Amen.

6

The Power of Loving Your Husband

Team Building Through Love

Wives, submit to your husbands as to the Lord.
—Eph. 5:22

Yvonne Continues

*H*ave you noticed that sex to your husband is different than it is for you? For example, how often does he think about sex compared to how often you think about it? I know, I know—some of you think that's *all* he ever thinks about. I once asked Bob if it's true that sex is all that men think about. He responded, "No, we think about two or three other things too."

OK, he was kidding me, but men do have a much stronger sex drive than women. The urge that hits him is something that is programmed inside of his body. He didn't create that urge—God did. When a man's seminal vesicles are full, a nerve impulse is triggered in his brain for both a need and a desire for sexual release. He doesn't control those internal mechanisms of his. It's simply the way he was created.

Now the external release is, of course, up to him and his wife to negotiate. For the average American male the urge hits about every three days. I can just hear a newlywed ask, "Don't you mean every three *hours?*" or an "oldy"-wed asking, "Don't you mean every three *months?*" Of course there are many variables involved here, because everyone's physiology is different.

Sex for a husband is more than just a physical release. The way he sees himself as a man is tied to his sexuality, and he's very vulnerable in this area. That's why your sexual response to him is very important. The way you respond to his advances and the enjoyment you show when making love with him thus affirms his masculinity.

That's why a man who suffers from impotence will start to feel as though he's less than a man. It hits him personally and hits him hard. That's why your husband should seek help if it happens to him, for 80 percent of impotency problems can be cured.

I've asked men in my men's-only session, "If you could tell your wives just one thing about your sexual relationship, what would it be?" The one comment that has surfaced above all the others was that they want more than just a body to perform on. In their sexual union husbands don't want an attitude of "Are you done yet?" or "I'll let you have what you want if you'll just leave me alone for a couple of days." It tremendously frustrates a husband to think his wife is just putting up with him in bed.

A husband wants a wife who will respond to him. He wants to know that she's drawn to him and that he's capable of giving his wife pleasure. Too many wives think he's in the sex arena just for his own pleasure. Well, true—some men are, and that's a loss for both partners, but most husbands want to know that they're giving pleasure to their wives. Speaking frankly, a greater joy to a godly, masculine husband isn't his own release but rather seeing that his wife is satisfied and enjoying their sexual union. Does this surprise you? Just ask your husband.

That's why a wife who is her husband's complement, as we discussed in the previous chapter, needs to make time for lovemaking. It should become more of a priority to you as a wife. Too often we wives put all our effort and energy into our children, work, church, and community service. While these are important, they tend to drain our energy, which often leaves us zero energy for our husbands. Our schedules need to reflect this priority. When we say this to a group of newlyweds, they don't quite understand our meaning, but when we talk to couples who are raising children, they know exactly what we mean.

One word seems to dominate our life in child-rearing years, and that word is "tired"! This can also be the case, however, even when there are no children at home.

Burning the Candle at Both Ends

As I mentioned earlier, I became so busy with our work that I was burning my life's candle at both ends. Our love life was a low priority. This wasn't because I didn't enjoy it, because I did, but it was because I was too busy with so many other priorities. I realized I had to make this area a priority because I didn't want to put Bob in the position of feeling like a beggar, because I knew what would be next—he would stop approaching me. No matter what your age, make the time and plan the time for a sexual encounter. That might mean taking a nap to be more refreshed at night, or changing or cutting back on some of your schedule. It also means preparing yourself emotionally. Don't forget that the most significant sex organ is your *brain.* The more time we spend dwelling on the good facets of our husbands, the better prepared we'll be emotionally.

Also, don't be afraid to schedule your times together. We may say to each other, "Let's plan on Wednesday afternoon at 3:00 for a special time of intimacy." Does planning it like that take away the excitement? Not at all. It *heightens* the excitement. · When we do this for a day or two ahead of that time, we remind each other about our special rendezvous, and as Wednesday hits Bob asks the Lord for divine intervention to race the clock ahead a few hours. All this builds anticipation and excitement.

As I'm writing about making your lovemaking a priority in your life, I know there are some female readers who are thinking, "I understand what you're saying, and I don't disagree with it, but I have absolutely no desire for sex." More and more, this dilemma is plaguing both men and women. Much of it has to do with the stress we're all under, but for women there can also be a number of other different ingredients in the mix. If that's true, an important quest is to find an answer for it, because God created women to have a sexual desire, and there's a reason it's not being experienced.

Some of those reasons can be psychological, perhaps in which there was physical or sexual abuse in the past. Or perhaps there was a wrongful influence by a father or mother (usually the mother) so the daughter grew up with a distorted view of sex and sexual pleasure. Another reason can be anger or resentment toward the mate. All these areas influence a desire level.

Some of it can be identified as lifestyle choices, such as not getting adequate sleep, not exercising, eating a poor diet of foods high in fat and sugar but low in fiber and other important nutrients that feed the body. And if these choices have brought on additional weight gain, they can affect sexual desire.

Some of the loss of sexual desire is due to physical reasons, such as taking certain medications. It could be caused by an imbalance in the thyroid or adrenal glands. It could be that hormones are out of whack, and a woman doesn't have to be in the menopause age for this to happen. It could be that she is low in estrogen or even testosterone. Even a hysterectomy that removes the ovaries causes the body to go into hormone shock.

All these factors and more affect our sexual desire. I encourage any woman who can raise her hand to one or more of the above not to give in and just live with these facts, but rather to find an answer. It may take some detective work, but it's well worth the effort.

Wife to Wife

We as wives want our husbands to talk to us and share with us their thoughts, dreams, and feelings. But the only way they'll open up to us is when there's a safe environment in which to do so. That comes when they learn to trust us because they know we're loyal to them. By following the guidelines to be a champion wife as outlined in the previous chapter, this will be developed. To better help us be our husbands' cheerleaders, champions, companions, or complements, there are some things we can do.

1. Let the Lord Work Through You

To do all that I have written about will be impossible unless you allow the Lord to do it through you. A verse to claim for this thought is Col. 1:27: "Christ in you, the hope of glory." Commit yourself to loving your husband God's way—not your way, but God's way. That means "dying to self" daily and surrendering your will for Him to work in you. That also means that when you notice certain things *not* being resolved, you'll remember that the Lord is your strength and shield (Ps. 28:7).

2. *Be Careful What You Fill Your Mind With*

Surround yourself with others who hold marriage in high esteem. Being around others, especially women, who berate marriage or the male sex will adversely affect your attitude toward your mate. Other things that can affect our attitude are romance novels and television soap operas. I'm not saying you cannot read or view them, but ask yourself the question "Does this material or program make me feel satisfied with my relationship with my husband or dissatisfied? And if Jesus were with me right now, would I ask Him to join me in reading this book or watching this program?"

I had to take that approach years ago when I watched a particular soap opera. I rationalized that being an adult, this program couldn't have much of an influencing factor in my life. I was wrong and became aware of being negative toward Bob. He never seemed to match up to the perfect heroes on this show who said all the perfect lines. How could he? The soap characters were not real. At least Bob was real.

What thoughts fill your mind all day? Are they positive thoughts about your mate, or negative ones? Pray that God will open your eyes to his good qualities. Often I've found that a quality we might consider negative can actually be turned around to be positive. After saying that to a female friend of mine, she replied, "You're right. I've often thought of my husband as not being as exciting as I think he should be, since he's so predictable. If I look at that in a positive vein, I can see him as dependable and trustworthy—and those are qualities I admire and am thankful for."

Write down those good qualities. Focus on them. Pray about them. Thank God for them. Allow God to change your attitude.

3. *Practice Good Self-Talk*

Self-talk is the talk you have with yourself all day. Most of it is silent, inside your mind. We're often led to believe that outside events or people affect our attitudes and feelings more than self-talk. Not true. It's the other way around. Our emotions start in our mind and grow into feelings of worry, anger, and happiness.

Our self-talk is so automatic that we're mostly unaware we're even doing it. Our self-talk can be positive or negative. A lot of negative self-talk makes you a negative person. Emerson said, "Be aware of what you set your mind on, for that you will surely become."

Our self-talk affects the way we act toward our mate. Here's an example for you: You and your husband have planned a night out, but at the last minute he calls and says, "Sorry, but the boss just gave me a project due tomorrow morning. That means I have to stay and work late tonight. What I'd like to do, Honey, is switch our plans to tomorrow night. OK?" You hang up and begin your self-talk:

Didn't he know I had looked forward to this night all week? I bet he didn't even think about me when he accepted the project. He could have told his boss no, that he had an important engagement with his wife. I bet he likes being at work more than being with me and even volunteered to work late so he wouldn't have to go out with me tonight. I know he doesn't care about me. I guess I'm not worthwhile enough to care about. In fact, nobody cares about me. Oh, why did I ever marry that man?

By the time you finish with your self-talk, you're depressed and mad at your husband because you believe he doesn't think being with you is worthwhile. Guess what—in most cases your thoughts aren't even close to being true.

So what do you do?

Step 1: Capture the Thought

2 Cor. 10:5 says, "We capture every thought and make it give up and obey Christ" (NCV). Often we don't do this. We just let our thoughts go on and on and on, and our thinking starts to imprison us. Tune in to your own self-talk, and when you hear it going negative, *stop it.*

Step 2: Challenge the Thought

When your self-talk is negative it's usually emotionally charged, plus exaggerated—and let's toss in overgeneralized and illogical. That's why we need to challenge it.

The best way I've found to challenge the thought is to talk it out loud or write it down. Do it either way, but get it out. The longer it stays in your mind, the more it gets distorted. When it's out, we often can "see the light." If you write it down, divide a piece of paper in two. On the left side write all the reasons you believe the thought is true, and on the right side jot down all the reasons you believe it's false, relying on the Holy Spirit to show you the truth.

Ask yourself some questions about what you've just told yourself:

- Is it true?
- How do I know it's true?
- Why should I believe this?
- Am I overreacting?
- What's the real issue?

Step 3: Change the Thought

After challenging your self-talk, you need to reflect on the truth. Replace your self-talk with right thoughts. Reading scripture can help you get refocused. Phil. 4:8 tells us what we need to focus on: "Whatever is true, whatever is noble, whatever is right, whatever is pure, whatever is lovely, whatever is admirable—if anything is excellent or praiseworthy—think about such things." Godly thoughts and godly thinking patterns have the ability to transform the way we deal with our mates.

Doing these things will help us be the woman spoken about in Prov. 31:10-12: "If you can find a truly good wife, she is worth more than precious gems! Her husband can trust her, and she will richly satisfy his needs. She will not hinder him, but help him all her life" (TLB).

TEAM-BUILDING QUESTIONS

1. What are some things in your daily schedule that tend to zap your energy most? List them, and then consider whether they directly or indirectly affect your sex life with your husband.

_____

_____

_____

_____

2. From your list of energy-zappers, think of alternative approaches. Are there any daily duties that you could trade off with another mom in your neighborhood? Could any of your "daily" duties become "two or three times a week" duties in order to conserve time and energy? What are some other options for you?

3. Do you have any friends who habitually downgrade men, especially their own husbands, in the company of other women? If so, consider being the one who turns the next such conversation in another direction—maybe even say something sweet about your own husband.

Team-Building Action Steps

1. List every good quality you can find in your husband in the next five days.

_____	_____	_____
_____	_____	_____
_____	_____	_____
_____	_____	_____
_____	_____	_____

Review the list after five days. Do you feel better about him as your husband? If not, spend special, private time in prayer about your relationship, and listen—really listen—to what God wants you to do about your negative feelings.

2. Check your own self-talk over the next 24 hours to see if it's more negative or more positive. If you're leaning toward more negative self-talk, then record here your response to the three steps that can help you break the habit of negative self-talk. Choose one of your thoughts:

(1) Capture the thought _____

_____

_____

(2) Challenge the thought_____

_____

_____

(3) Change the thought _____

_____

_____

Father, thank You for helping me see
the deep needs of my husband and giving me
the inner desire to meet those needs.
With Your help, Father, I'll focus on his good qualities
and allow You to take care of the rest.
In Jesus' name. Amen.

Building Block No. 3

Communication

7

Help! My Mate Can't Read My Signals!

Team Building Through Communication

> *Communication is depositing a part*
> *of yourself in another person.*
> —Anonymous

We communicate from the moment we get a pat on the rump from the doctor until the moment it's time to leave this world. Since we're always communicating, the process should be easy, right? Maybe not. It's one of the most difficult areas in all relationships—especially in a marriage.

A couple was celebrating their 50th wedding anniversary. When it came time for them to make a little speech, family and friends gathered around them. Now the wife had become hard of hearing in the last five years, and it was a sore spot for hubby. He approached his wife, made some complementary remarks, and said, "My beloved wife has been faithful to me these 50 golden years. She is tried and true."

As he reached to give her a little hug, she said, "What?"

"I said—and pay close attention since everybody is watching and listening—that you've been so faithful to me these 50 golden years. You are tried and true."

Once again he reached to give her a hug, but her response was to shout, "Speak up, Harry! I cain't hear ya!"

Thoroughly frustrated now, he glared at her and yelled,

"Read my lips. I'm saying that you've been a faithful wife, so tried and true."

She then nodded, and shouted, "Oh, I hear ya. Well, I'm tired of you too!"

Slight misunderstanding.

Reminds us of the axiom "I know you believe you understand what you think I said, but I'm not sure you realize that what you heard is not what I meant."

In a study done with hundreds of divorced couples, the question was asked as to what they felt was the contributing factor that led to their divorce. Eighty-six percent of them said it was because of communication problems.

That reminds us of a cartoon in which a sad-faced couple said to a marriage counselor, "Actually, our *in*ability to communicate is the only thing we have in common." What a night-and-day difference from the hour they exchanged their wedding vows! Most could communicate on *anything* then, but as the months turned into years, their inclination was to disagree on *everything*.

Why do communication problems cause so many marriages to fail? Because communication in marriage functions as the pathway to intimacy. As we pointed out earlier in this book, God said in Gen. 2:18, "It is not good for the man to be alone. I will make a helper suitable for him." And in Mark 10:8, "The two will become one flesh. So they are no longer two, but one." As we learn from these two verses, marriage was created to overcome man's loneliness problem. Two individuals with their differences are coming together to complement each other by becoming one flesh. They will develop closeness in marriage by sharing with each other their ideas, thoughts, and feelings. So if communication breaks down, they naturally notice a wall between them. Eventually they will feel isolated from each other as the wall continues to grow.

We know that most, if not all, couples are like us in that we desire to communicate and share our lives with each other, but we find circumstances that can trip us up. Those are what we call "stumbling blocks." The following are the four most common ones. See if any of them apply to your marriage.

Television

Watching television can be a fun joint time together when you talk about what you viewed and what you learned. However, far too many couples just sit and watch the boob tube, not communicating, just running into the kitchen for fattening snacks during the commercials, then turning it off and ambling off to bed. An entire noncommunication evening slips by and fades into the night.

After many years of the above, we have learned to limit the amount of our television watching.

Fatigue

Some people are "morning" people, which means, of course, that others are "night" people. Usually opposites marry each other. Did you?

For example, it's 6 A.M. The alarm goes off. What does Morning Person do? He or she flies out of bed singing, "This is the day, this is the day that the Lord has made . . ." and rushes over to click on the TV set so the day can start with leaping around the room to the encouragement of Ms. Glistening Sweat hosting the "Pre-Dawn Hurt-Your-Body Show."

Night Person continues to lie as still as a fossilized tree—can't even open one eye—and mumbles, barely audible, "Please get me some coffee and pour it directly into my eyes." Night Person really gets cranking around 12:00 noon, when fully awake, and can work tirelessly until 2:00 in the morning. Morning Person is usually falling asleep by 8:30 at night. In this one-is-a-morning-person-one-is-a-night-person marriage, pillow talk late at night is not going to work. Yvonne found this out early in our marriage.

Yvonne: *I remember when we were first married, for the first three months I fell asleep crying about every night. I thought Bob didn't love me and didn't want to talk with me. When I grew up, as a little girl, I shared my bedroom with my sister. We'd go to bed at night and talk, talk, talk until we fell asleep. Then when I went to college I had roommates, and we'd talk, talk, talk until we fell asleep. When I got married I was so excited to think that now I had a husband who, when we went to bed, would talk, talk, talk until we, too, would fall asleep. I was shocked and hurt to discover that three minutes after going to bed he was sound asleep. So I would silently cry until I fell asleep.*

Bob: *Men, there are two reasons we go to bed at night, right? Wink-wink. Well, since the first one wasn't going to happen, then I applied the second reason and fell asleep. Made sense to me.*

Yvonne: *I finally figured out that my timing was off. Bob* *worked hard during the day and was very tired at night, so he would immediately fall asleep. But during the day, conversations were free-flowing. Now that I think back on those early days, I just shake my head and laugh.*

We finally realized we needed to find another time to be able to interact effectively.

Children

Now it's not that children set out to intentionally squeeze any adult conversation out of you, but they sure let their needs be known immediately, don't they? As a loving parent, it's hard to ignore them. Conversations during child-rearing years are devoted either directly *to* the kids or somehow *about* the kids. Keep this in mind: if you don't find time to talk with each other during those years your children are at home, after they fly the coop you'll find you don't have a relationship with each other.

The Rat Race

Couples talk, but their conversations often seem to be centered around such deep, intimate subjects as

"What time did you say I needed to pick up the kids?"

"We need to take the car in for an oil change. What day's best for you?"

"What hotel will you be staying in at next week's conference?"

For many, in today's rat race it seems that everything is either urgent, critical, important, or immediate, and sometimes they all seem to be interwoven. Many couples no longer have time for important discussions or dreaming together with their "What ifs." Finding the time for conversations is a key.

As we were struggling to communicate with each other, we found in our own marriage that we were getting hung up over those four stumbling blocks. We didn't feel the way we were communicating was building a team. On the contrary, we felt we were on opposing teams, each trying to score against the other. We knew that in order to be teammates, we needed to make a change in our communication. We started with three principles:

Principle No. 1—Communicate so they will understand.

Principle No. 2—Talk so others will listen.

Principle No. 3—Listen so others will talk.

They sound so simple, but they're absolutely vital for good

communication. Let's look at each principle—No. 1 in this chapter, Nos. 2 and 3 in the next chapter.

Principle No. 1—Communicate So They Will Understand

Ever notice how men and women use language so differently? They speak on two different wavelengths. One speaks F.M. and the other speaks A.M. Ever notice, too, that men don't talk the same way to women as they do to other men? In some cases, at least, they'd better not!

It's like the man who just punched the work clock. With 10 minutes left before he starts his shift, he ambles over to the coffeepot, pours a cup, takes a sip, and then spits it out and grumbles, "Hey—who made this slop?"

A man standing next to him says, "I did. If you don't like it, make your own."

Now, ladies, this may be hard for you to believe, but those guys aren't mad at each other. That exchange is no big deal. It's simply guy talk. That's one way men bond.

Bob: *But suppose it's a Sunday morning and my beloved and I are next to each other in our kitchen. I pour a cup of coffee, spit it out, and say, "Did you make this slop?" Gentlemen, am I in trouble, like big trouble? Can we agree that for the next 24 hours it could possibly be cold meals, cold bed? Just kidding, but it's true that in so many instances men don't talk the same way to women as we do to other men.*

We even use words differently.

Yvonne: *For example, I could say to Bob, "How was dinner tonight?"*

Bob: *"Fine."*

Yvonne: *"Just 'fine'?"*

Bob: *"Yeah, I liked it. It was fine."*

Yvonne: *"What was wrong with it?"*

Bob: *"Nothing was wrong with it. Aren't you listening to me? I said it was fine."*

Yvonne: *"Well, if you didn't like it, you should have told me halfway through dinner and I would have fixed something else."*

Bob: *"What?"*

Yvonne: *Wives, what does "fine" mean to you? Probably the same as it means to me. It was sorta OK. So-so.*

Bob: *Men, doesn't the word "fine" mean* fine?*—as in "good"? As in "real good"? Evidently not. No, what Yvonne really wanted to hear was "The table setting was outstanding, the cuisine scrumptious, and I want to make passionate love to the chef." Something on that or-der.*

Or how about this one?

Yvonne: *"Can I talk to you for a minute?"*

Bob: *Guys, correct me if I'm wrong, but doesn't "a minute" mean 60 seconds? So when she talks 60 seconds into history, I get a bit edgy and wonder why the chat isn't drawing to a quick close.*

Yvonne: *Women know that a minute is really however long it takes to finish what I want to say, and now that I have his attention I should toss in a few more subjects before he gets that glazed look over his eyes. Right?*

Since men are information oriented, they take words more literally than women. As another example, consider how a man reacts if his wife were to say, "You *never* take me out to dinner." He hears the words that sound like an accusation to him, and he wants to correct them by countering with "How can you say that? I took you out about four months ago." But she's coming from a different point of view.

Women use words to express emotions and will amplify certain words to express feelings. When she says "never" or "al-ways," she rarely means them literally. She's saying in her own way that something isn't happening, and she wants to make sure you understand how important it is to her. Unfortunately, when we don't understand the perspective of our spouse, the result is an argument with no agreement in sight. She is arguing her feelings. She feels her feelings are being discounted when he tries to correct her. Now he's arguing the contents of her words, thinking that she tends to make a big deal out of every-thing. Sound familiar? So what do you do with your differ-ences?

As a couple we keep in mind the words of Phil. 2:3-7. The following is our personal "Turnbull paraphrase" as we relate these verses to husbands and wives: *"Husbands and wives,* do nothing out of selfish ambition or vain conceit, but in humility consider *your spouse* better than yourself. Each of you *married couples* should look not just to your own interests, but also to the interests of *your mate.* Your attitudes should be the same as that of Christ Jesus, who being in very nature God . . . took the very nature of a servant. *So, husbands and wives, serve one another."*

We used to deal with our communication differences in an attitude of "Sorry 'bout that, but that's just the way I am. Take it or leave it—I'm not changing." With that selfish attitude, no wonder we had so many misunderstandings.

That was then. This is now. We now have the attitude that's described in Phil. 2—one that says, "Let me understand you better. What areas can I change in that will help improve our communication?" What a big difference this has made for us! We don't know if we'll ever totally understand each other, but that's OK. At least we're *trying* to understand each other, and we do it now with a fun attitude rather than an adversarial one.

So how do you practically live out Phil. 2 in your communication? We're going to provide some examples of male-female differences. After each one we'll explain how you can learn to meet each other's needs through your differences. Keep in mind that when we say men do this and women do that, we're making some generalities. Eighty to 85 percent will fit within those generalities; 15 to 20 percent may not. That's all right, because our communication styles are affected by a lot more than just male-female differences. In the mix are also our personalities, upbringing, and experiences. We're a complex mixture of all these. More than likely you will see yourself in some of these examples.

Highlighter and Detailer

Bob is a *highlighter* and Yvonne is a *detailer*.

Bob: *Yvonne talked on the phone for two hours with her mom. She got off the phone and I walked by her, and silly me—you'd think I would have learned by now, but I asked, "What did your mom have to say?"*

Yvonne: *Well, since I talked with mom for two hours, of course I had so much to share with Bob—but do you think he was really interested in our conversation? No. How did I know? He went and turned the TV on.*

Bob: *Bad move.*

Bob wanted Yvonne's story edited down and wasn't interested in every small detail. He would often say, "Honey, is there a point to this story coming somewhere on the horizon?"

Bob was saying this because men are information gatherers. When they're listening to a conversation, they're thinking, "How can I use this information to fix something?" So they're looking for the bottom line—just the highlight. Also, that's why men often *float* while they're hearing a story from their wives—because they can't figure out what to do with this information.

While men are bottom-line highlighters, women are more like an encyclopedia, with lots of paragraphs, lots of details. Your wife gives lots of details because she wants to make sure you completely understand what she's saying. She's expressing feelings and sharing herself through communication. She does this because she sees herself as part of a network of connections and relationships. Intimacy is key for her. So when she communicates with her husband, she's not just dispensing information, but sharing her life. That's a way to feel closer to him.

These differences can account for this type of conversation. Bob had just hung up the telephone from having talked with his mother.

Yvonne: *What did your mom have to say?*
Bob: *She's taking another trip down into Baja.*
Yvonne: *When is she going?*
Bob: *I don't know.*
Yvonne: *Well, how long is she going to stay?*
Bob: *I'm not sure.*
Yvonne: *Didn't you ask her?*
Bob: *No, I didn't think it was important to know. I figured if she wanted me to know she would have told me.*
Yvonne: *Well, is she over her cold yet?*
Bob: *I guess so. She didn't mention it.*
Yvonne: *And, of course, you didn't ask.*
Bob: *I didn't think it was important to know. If she wasn't OK, I'm sure she would have told me.*

See what we mean? A woman will ask questions to show her concern and show she cares, plus women want the details to add to the flavor of the conversation. A man asks questions to receive information so he can either fix something or complete a task. If the info isn't relevant to him, he figures, "Why ask?"

Our solution is living out the Phil. 2 verses. What Bob has

done to meet Yvonne's needs is to find out more information, especially when he talks to his mom, and pass it along to her, using more adjectives, not just giving the bottom line.

An example of Bob's efforts goes back to when we lived in Hawaii. Bob officiated at nearly 200 weddings. Yvonne rarely went with him since she didn't know the people—mostly tourists—getting married. When Bob would come home she would ask how the wedding went, and he would say the usual "Fine." She would then ask, "What did the bride wear?" Laughing, he would answer, "Clothes. You know I insist the bride and groom wear clothes." It finally dawned on Bob that Yvonne was interested not only in how the wedding went, but some details about it—especially what the bride wore. This was of interest to her.

Bob finally thought, "I'm just being selfish. I need to remember more details and pass them along to Yvonne—I know it interests her and would please her."

The next wedding was a formal outdoor event featuring a rather unusual romantic setting—inside a dormant volcano known as Diamond Head. Bob checked with the bridesmaid and asked her to give him all the "technical" terms for the bride's wedding gown. Upon returning home, Yvonne asked her usual, "How was the wedding?" Bob gave his usual "Fine." Yvonne responded with her usual second line, "What did the bride wear?" While walking past Yvonne into the bedroom, Bob recited exactly what the bride wore. When he finished, Yvonne laughed and shouted, "You really do love me!" What was Bob's reaction? "Is communication in a marriage *this easy*? I've got it made!"

Now let's flip-flop this and see what Yvonne has done to meet Bob's needs.

Yvonne: *I've learned to talk newspaper style to Bob. A newspaper article is fashioned after a pyramid. First come the most important highlights of the story, followed by more details, and then others, all in descending order of importance. Increasingly minute details are provided the farther on down into the story you read. So I start with the major point of the story and then add details. I keep on adding details until I see a glazed look start to come over his eyes. When that happens, I know he has heard all he wants and needs to hear. If I want to share more details, I'll go call a friend of mine.*

We remember the day Yvonne agreed to focus on meeting

Bob's needs in conversation. Yvonne chose a humorous approach to get her point across.

Bob: *That night I was watching "Nightline" on TV, half on the couch and half on the floor. Yvonne waited until the commercial came on, then walked between me and the TV set, paused dramatically in front of me, and said, "Wife wearing new nightgown. Film at 11." That headline certainly got my attention. I said nighty-night to Ted Koppel, jumped up from the couch, and flexed my Tarzan muscles, saying, "I want my Jane!" One problem—I smelled like Cheetah and needed a shower. But she surely got my attention with her headline approach.*

Making Requests—Making Suggestions

Men make requests. Women make suggestions. A couple driving home together after a long trip could have a conversation something like this:

Wife: "Would you like to stop and get something to eat?"

Husband: "No. I'm not hungry."

Wife: "Are you sure you aren't hungry?"

Husband: "Yeah, I'm sure. I want to get home and see the Lakers' game."

During the remainder of the trip the wife is disappointed and sits in silence. After a while, noticing the silence, the husband speaks.

Husband: "Is there something wrong?"

Wife: "No, I guess not."

Husband: "OK."

They arrive home, unpack the car, and the wife spends the rest of the evening sighing and sulking, hoping the husband will pick up on her subtle cues. After a few hours, she realizes he isn't picking them up. Finally she decides to say something.

Wife: "Tonight I wanted to spend a little more time with you. I wanted to stop on the way home and get something to eat."

Husband: "Well, why didn't you say so?"

Wife: "I thought you knew what I wanted when I asked if you would like something to eat."

The solution is again living out the verses in Phil. 2. Don't make assumptions that he should know what you need and want. One of the funniest overheads we use in our seminars shows a husband and wife in a bed, both leaning up against their pillows with folded arms and the husband saying, "Apparently I've done something to upset you." The funny part is seeing the two big strands of coiled barbed wire running down the middle of the bed. Yes, apparently!

Wives, he isn't picking up on all the verbal and nonverbal cues you're giving him. His brain is wired to be focused. Remember his compartments? It's not that he doesn't want to do something for you; it's just that he isn't aware of what you want unless you make it very clear to him. *Tell him.*

And men, knowing that she often gives verbal cues of what she would like, start listening for her *suggestions,* such as "Can you . . . ?" or "Would you like . . . ?" Those actually mean "I would like you to . . ."

It's like when Yvonne says, "The wastebasket's full."

Bob: *I've learned that she's not just giving me a piece of information, but instead she is asking me to empty the garbage. Whoever said understanding each other would be easy?*

Giving Advice—Solving Problems

When a mate has a problem, everyone deals with it differently.

When a husband has a problem, the wife often wants to help by giving him advice. Instead of being pleased, he often gets upset with her and may even retreat from her.

Debra: "Honey, you know, if you would just take some more computer courses it would help your chances of advancement at your job."

Shawn: "I don't want to take more courses."

Debra: "But it would help. You need to consider that we need more money, and this is one way you could get it."

Shawn: "Get off my back. I think I do just fine providing for the family."

Debra: "Yes, you do, but this will just help us all the more."

[Silence]

Debra: "Well, what do you think?"

[Silence]

Debra: "Shawn, aren't you listening to me?"

[Shawn leaves the room.]

Debra feels very frustrated and doesn't understand what just happened.

We need to look at this situation through the prism of the way a man functions in the world and the way a woman does. In a woman's world, giving advice and help to another woman indicates that you care about her. But in a man's world, giving advice and help to another man might be seen as an indication that the recipient is incompetent. A fear many a man has is that he's not good enough, that he'll fail. So he's constantly proving himself to those around him. If his wife is giving him unsolicited advice, he thinks his feared failure is coming true, so he feels controlled, possibly humiliated.

Our solution—again living out those verses in Philippians. Yvonne has learned to do something with Bob. Before she offers any advice, she'll preface it with "Would you like to hear a suggestion I have?" Sometimes he says yes, and when that occurs Yvonne states her suggestion, but in a manner that doesn't make him think he can't handle things. She uses a number of techniques. If she asks the above question but Bob says, "Not now," she doesn't badger him to say yes, but drops it. She'll say, "If you'd like to hear my suggestion later, let me know."

Wives, this is really important to learn. The other way makes him feel he's on the defense all the time, so he won't be open to your suggestions. Since Yvonne has learned to "drop it" if Bob doesn't want her suggestion, this is now what occurs:

Yvonne: *Bob will now come to me when he's dealing with something and ask for my advice. Before, he would rarely ask, even if he wanted it. I don't threaten him now, so he's open to hear from me.*

When a wife has a problem, the husband wants to solve it. She often gets frustrated and accuses him of not understanding.

Tess: "I can't believe all the things I have to get done this week. I never have any time for myself."

Rush: "You should quit your job so you'd have more time to do all the things you want to do. You don't have to work so hard or put in those long hours."

Tess: "You don't understand. I like my job, but I still have so much to do here at home. I can't seem to do it all."

Rush: "Hey—I help around the house. Do you want me to do more?"

Tess: "No, I'm not asking you to do more, but I just can't do it all."

Rush: "The house doesn't have to look perfect. Who cares?"

Tess: "*I* care. It's important to me. I wish you'd listen to me."

Rush: "I *am* listening to you. You listen to *me.* I'm trying to solve this for you."

Tess: "I'm not asking you to solve this for me."

Rush: "If you don't want me to solve it, then why are you telling me this?"

Tess: "I just want some understanding."

They both walk away not understanding each other. What happened here?

Two women will discuss problems in order to get closer to each other, not necessarily to arrive at solutions. Tess just wanted Rush to listen to her, be a sounding board, a supportive friend.

Rush put on his "Mr. Fix It" hat, because his sense of self is defined by his ability to solve problems and get results. A man will try to solve a problem by himself and will ask for help only when he's unable to solve it. So he believes, "If she tells me something, she must want it fixed. Otherwise why would she tell me?" But by solving it when she didn't want it solved, she believes that her feelings were being discounted, and that hurt her.

Our solution is once again to apply those Philippians verses. When Yvonne is telling Bob something and Bob isn't sure whether she just wants him to listen to her or to listen to solve it, we've cleared that up with a mutually agreeable action.

Bob will put up his hand and say, "Do you want solution or sympathy?" If Yvonne says, "Sympathy," Bob usually mumbles "Ah, nuts!" under his breath, but since he has agreed to sympathetically listen, he abides by it. Fortunately for Mr. "I Really Want to Fix It," more often than not Yvonne's conclusion includes a request to help solve it. Whew!

Now it's your turn. In what areas are the two of you constantly arguing? Rethink what your original responses were and how you could make a change in your future responses using Phil. 2:3-7. We know by our own experiences, and you will, too, that by applying those verses there will be a big difference in helping you understand each other.

Team-Building Questions

1. Of the four stumbling blocks that were written about in this chapter—television, fatigue, children, and the rat race—which do you find has the biggest impact on your marriage? How does it affect it? Do you need to do something to change it? If so, discuss ways to make those changes.
2. We discussed in this chapter that men and women speak on different wavelengths. Discuss a recent event in your marriage relationship that was a result of different ways you both use language.
3. Has what you read in this chapter given you a different perspective on that situation? What is it?
4. Will learning that there are real differences in the way we all communicate help you communicate any differently with your mate? How?
5. There may be other differences, aside from male/female, that may be impacting your marriage. If there are, discuss them with your spouse. Look at them from both a negative and a positive point of view.

Team-Building Action Steps

1. This week pick one communication difference you have found that you continually have conflict over. Work out a solution for that problem using Phil. 2:3-7 as your underlying attitude.
2. Look at the following verses in Proverbs. Think about how you can practically apply them to your communication.

Prov. 11:9, 12-13
Prov. 15:1
Prov. 15:4
Prov. 15:28
Prov. 18:13
Prov. 18:15
Prov. 20:19
Prov. 25:11
Prov. 29:20

Father, help me to communicate so that
my mate can read my signals.

8

Why Can't We Talk to Each Other?

TEAM BUILDING THROUGH ENERGIZING COMMUNICATION

*Knowing when to say nothing
is 50 percent of tact and 90 percent of marriage.*
—Sydney Harris

*O*ur words are like seeds that we plant in our mate and family members. They are powerful. Through the spoken word God created the world. Since our words are powerful, we need to ask ourselves what type of seeds we're planting—seeds of weeds or seeds of beautiful flowers?

Yvonne: *Several years ago, when I stopped talking long enough, I realized that Bob wasn't talking very much to me, other than "safe" comments about how our lawn was growing and something about the weather. I finally asked him why.*

Bob: *I said, "Do you really want to know?"*

Yvonne: *Yes, I really do. What's wrong?*

Bob: *I don't talk much with you anymore because every time I say almost anything, and I'm not exaggerating, you immediately give me your "C & C" routine—correct and criticize. Yeah, that's it—you correct and criticize everything I say, so I've pretty well lost interest in talking to you about anything.*

Yvonne: *Do you know what I wanted to do right then? That's right—correct and criticize him. But I didn't. Something stopped me. It's hard to explain, but it was as if an invisible hand went over my* *mouth to keep it shut. Talking is one of my biggest problems, as I'm a true extrovert. Whatever is in my brain comes out of my mouth without a whole lot of thinking. I often leave a room asking myself, "Why did I say that?"*

As I listened to what Bob was saying, I came under the conviction of the Holy Spirit and realized that Bob was 100 percent right. I had been tearing down my relationship with the words I spoke. I was not letting God control my conversations. I had become a planter of weeds in my husband's life. I apologized to Bob, and we started working on a change in my speech pattern. I now take to heart the scripture found in Ps. 141:3: "Set a guard over my mouth, O LORD; keep watch over the door of my lips." There are times when I ask the Lord to put a padlock on the door.

To be a seed planter of flowers instead of weeds, we found we needed to implement the next principle.

Principle No. 2—Talk So Others Will Listen

Yvonne discovered she was not talking to Bob in such a way to cause him to *want* to listen. In fact, it caused him to close his ears and retreat from her. But Scripture expresses the power of positive communication, or one could say *energized* communication. Our own husband-and-wife paraphrase of Eph. 4:29 reads, *"Husbands and wives, when you talk to each other* do not let any unwholesome talk come out of your mouth, but only what is helpful for building *your spouse* up according to *his or her* needs, that it may benefit *your mate who is listening to you."*

From this verse we have found some practical insights that we have put into our marriage. It has made a significant change in our relationship.

In the verse above, "unwholesome talk" is mentioned. What does that mean? Does that really have an effect on your mate? In the original language, "unwholesome" had the meaning of spoiled, decayed matter. Now doesn't that sound appetizing? It has a scent of death. It's the same way with our words when we speak unwholesome talk. It's as if we are speaking death to our mate. Prov. 18:21 says, "The tongue has the power of life and death"—not necessarily physical death, but emotional death.

That's what happened to Phillip and Jodie's marriage of 12

years. Jodie came to us and informed us that she wanted out of her marriage. She said, "Phillip is always telling me how stupid I am when I say something. If I take action to do something, he always makes a remark that he hopes I don't foul it up because I can't do things right. In the beginning of our marriage I would stick up for myself, but he would always argue me down until he felt he had won. After a few years I realized that defending myself didn't get me anywhere, so I decided to silently endure his constant negative put-downs. But after a while, I found myself starting to believe what he was saying about me. I was beginning to feel that I couldn't do anything right. The love I used to have for him has long ago disappeared. It's hard to love someone who gives me so much pain by his cutting words. Right now I'm so emotionally dead that I've decided the only way to survive is to get out of this marriage."

Phillip's words did not bring life to his wife; they brought death. Our words have the power to hurt or heal a relationship. How awful to see a marriage destroyed because of thoughtless selection of words!

What are some of the "unwholesome" words?

- Sarcasm and put-downs: "You want to try out for the soccer team? You've got to be kidding. You're so uncoordinated you'll have all your teammates laughing at you, and you'll just embarrass yourself—and us too."
- Exaggerated words: "You're so thoughtless. You never take me out to dinner anymore. Never."
- Nagging words: "Yeah, right—you'll get around to washing the car. Sure—just like you've done in getting around to mowing the lawn that's now higher than our house. Can't you ever do these things without me having to ask you over and over and over?"
- Cutting words: "Can't you ever do anything right?"

These types of reckless words can pierce people just like a sword (Prov. 12:18). Those words just plain hurt, as well as undermine a person's self-confidence. It causes him or her to want to give up. In order to escape the pain, the person will draw back, first from activities, then from his or her spouse. You can actually see this in Phillip and Jodie's situation. Unfortunately, their story doesn't have a happy ending, because their words left too many scars.

The following story gives a good visual example of scarring words:

A young boy grew up on a farm. Every time he said something naughty, he was told to pound a nail into the barn door. For each time he said something nice he could pull out one of the nails. Finally, at the age of 30, he had pulled out the last nail he had pounded into the barn door. As he stood back and looked at the door, to his horror he saw hundreds of holes. Those were the scars of his words he left on that door.

If *you* have come to realize that you've been planting seeds of weeds in your mate's life, you can change it, but it's going to take time. As with any weed in your garden, you can see the outer part of it—but below the surface there may be a deep system with many hidden seeds. You have to make sure you don't just use your weed-whacker to clip off the outer part and then think the weeds are gone. You have to dig out the root system. Helping that process along will be to ask forgiveness from your mate, and then each time a weed seems to crop up, deal with it immediately and make the proper correction. You want to replace those weeds with the next part of Eph. 4:29—speaking words that will be helpful in building up your mate. These words are what we call our "seeds of flowers." Life springs forth from them. Here are some ways:

- *Offering compliments.* Mark Twain said, "I can live for two months on a good compliment." Let's hope your mate doesn't have to wait that long for your compliments, but they still can keep you going. Say something like "You did a great job hanging that wallpaper. It looks terrific."
- *Offering words of praise.* The word "praise" comes from a Latin word for "worth." When you give praise to your mate, you're saying that you think he or she is worthwhile. "I appreciate all the hard work you did on that last project. That meant a lot to me."
- *Offering words of encouragement.* "Encouragement" means to incite someone in a given direction. You want to speak words that will help your mate become all that God intends for him or her to be. "Honey, I know you can do it. I'll be right here to support you any way I can." "I admire the way you hung in there when losing those 15 pounds seemed so hard. You're lookin' good."

As we write about positive words, we realize there can be barriers that prevent giving appreciation and encouragement.

1. An Attitude of "That's Just His [or Her] Job"

A wife may not express in words her appreciation when her husband takes out the trash every night, because she considers that it's his job, so why make a fuss over it? Don't take what your spouse does for granted. Let your spouse know of your thankfulness and appreciation frequently.

2. Lack of Role Models

A mate may have grown up in a family in which expressing appreciation was not part of the communication system, so he or she never learned how to do it. But when you realize how important energizing words are to your mate, you can learn to do it.

3. Fear of the Emotional Effects

The closeness that comes with expressing the positive can be threatening. This intimacy may make your mate feel a bit uncomfortable or anxious. The object in a marriage is to draw close to each other. What better way than to take a baby step in that direction through the thoughtful choice of your words?

If you're someone who has been neglecting to plant seeds of flowers, it may be difficult to even give one positive word a day. The starting point is really a change of attitude. Jesus said in Matt. 12:34, "Out of the overflow of the heart the mouth speaks."

Make a commitment to speak more kind, thoughtful, energizing words to your mate. Pray that God will change your focus to see what's right with your mate, and then start to speak those words. You're entering a process that will reinforce itself, but it starts with your first baby step.

To think before you speak takes simply stopping for a split second and considering if what you're going to say will be helpful for building others up. Our marriage paraphrase of 1 Thess. 5:14 would go like this: *"Husbands and wives, encourage and build your spouse up."*

Preface what you say by thinking about something that's credited to Martin Luther. When you're going to say something to someone, first ask yourself, "Will this be kind? Will it be necessary? Will it be true?" If it's not, why say it?

Remember Eph. 4:29? The section that says "according to their needs" means to be aware of our mate's needs and to give a response appropriate for the situation—a response that builds him or her up.

Example: Let's say hubby comes home from work to his wife, who is a busy stay-at-home mom with preschoolers. He comes through the door, and his frazzled wife says, "I've had a horribly exhausting day." What the husband should *not* say is "You think *you've* had a hard day—well, my day was even worse." That's a one-upmanship move. What he should do is set aside his rough day for a while and focus on both the Lord and his lady with words like, "I'm sorry your day was tough, but I'm home now. Let me jump in and grab those crazy kids for a while and give you a break." Meet the needs of your spouse with a servant's heart, just as Jesus came to us with a servant's heart.

The right words at the right time bring relief to a frazzled day. We find that in Prov. 15:23, "A man [or woman] finds joy in giving an apt reply—and how good is a timely word!"

Early in a marriage you often learn that there are times to say things and—you guessed it—times to say nothing. Often our timing isn't the best.

Bob: *We used to have a regularly scheduled argument on the mornings we were getting ready to travel to speak somewhere. The night before I would always ask Yvonne what time she would like the alarm to sound off. She always wanted a few more minutes of sleep, so she'd tell me what she would like the time to be, figuring she could be ready within that time frame before we had to head for the airport. Unfortunately, every time she'd be running 10 minutes late, so that was my cue to give her my famous lecture on how not to be late, how we need to get up earlier, and so on.*

Yvonne: *Well, I'd get all nervous and I'd launch into our standard on-the-way-to-the-airport argument.*

Bob: *After a few grumbling sessions together, it dawned on me that I wasn't using a godly approach to this matter. I became quite novel and asked, "Sweetie, is there something I can do to help you?" I stopped thinking about myself and focused on doing something to benefit her. That action took the pressure off, and we didn't end up in our usual argument.*

Yvonne: *Bob's actions also helped me to make a change. I realized I wasn't allowing myself enough time, so I needed to get up earlier.*

Timing is an area Yvonne struggles with. She's the type who wants to take care of things *when* she thinks of them. At times this is helpful, but at other times it ends up hurting the relationship.

Yvonne: *One example is when we're speaking and Bob says something I may not find appropriate. I used to immediately tell him during our first break. He was not highly receptive at that time. It would get him off track, and besides, it didn't need to be said right then. Now I wait, and later that night or maybe the next day I tell him about it if I still think it should be mentioned. He's more receptive then. However, sometimes after I think about it a little while, I discover that it really didn't need to be said. Now when I spot something that needs to be dealt with I first pray and ask God if this is the right time to bring it up. I've found that most of the time I receive a check from the Lord—it's not the right time. When you pray, God will help you wait for the right time to say it and the best possible way (Eccles. 3:7).*

When we make the change from planting seeds of weeds to seeds of flowers and say things that will meet each other's needs, then we'll see that our mate will listen when we speak.

Principle No. 3—Listen So Others Will Talk

The two most common complaints we hear are first, "People don't listen to me," and second, "People don't understand me."

Reminds us of the two psychiatrists who worked in the same office building. Every night when the young psychiatrist would leave the building, he was worn out and disheveled. But the 25-year veteran looked as fresh and chipper as when he first started work. After a few weeks of this, the new psychiatrist finally asked the older one as they walked into the parking lot, "How come you look so fresh and alive? I'm totally worn out after listening to my patients all day." The older psychiatrist just looked at him and said, "Who listens?"

That's a "ha-ha-ouch" story, for far too many people can identify with that. Their eyes may be looking at the person they're speaking with, but they're not listening. Too many are what we call "pretend listeners." They hear words and can even comment back to the speaker, but in reality they haven't understood what was being said, and 10 minutes later they have no idea what was told them. It's "in one ear and out the other."

We thought listening was something that came naturally. Silly us. Through our marriage we have found out differently. We're taught in James 1:19, "Everyone should be quick to listen, slow to speak and slow to become angry."

"Quick to listen" means more than just hearing words, but to *understand* what's being said. That's the key—listen to understand. We live in a world with billions of people, yet so many feel so isolated, and one of the contributing reasons to that is that we don't think people understand us. People are hungering to be listened to, to be understood.

There was once an advertisement in a Kansas newspaper that read, "For thirty minutes I will listen to you talk and give no comment. Cost is only $5.00." Guess what—the advertiser got *flooded* with calls from people who just wanted someone to listen to them.

When we've spoken to men who have had sexual affairs outside of marriage, we always ask them what they think caused them to do it. The vast majority of them said, in so many words, that it started with a woman who listened to what he had to say and showed a desire to understand him, which later led to illicit sexual intimacy.

A story we read helps make the point about listening. This true event happened many years ago in England. British statesman William Gladstone took a beautiful woman to dinner one night. The following night an equally distinguished opponent of Gladstone, Benjamin Disraeli, took her to dinner. After the two dinners she was asked her impression of the two men. She said, "When I left the dining room after sitting next to Mr. Gladstone, I thought he was the cleverest man in England. But after sitting next to Mr. Disraeli, I thought I was the cleverest woman in England."

Listening says, "I care. You are important. You are loved." We had a neighbor once whose five-year-old son ran into the kitchen one day saying, "Mom, you really love me."

Mom was pleased at this and said, "That's wonderful. I'd love to hear why you're saying that."

Her son said, "Because every time I want to talk to you, you put down whatever you're doing and listen to me."

Voltaire wrote, "The road to the heart is the ear."

Listening to one another is one of the most important skills we can develop. Many people have taken speech classes, but how many have taken a *listening* class? Most listening does not come naturally. We have noted some barriers to being a good listener.

1. Disinterest

An ancient philosopher named Zeno once said, "We have two ears and one mouth; therefore we should listen twice as much as we speak." Unfortunately, most people would rather talk than listen.

One time a father, mother, and their three children were having dinner. The oldest was a 16-year-old boy, followed by a 13-year-old daughter, with the caboose being a 7-year-old boy. All of a sudden the youngest yelled in his loudest voice, "Pass those potatoes!" Mom immediately scolded him and sent him to his room. He ran down the hall crying. Mom said, "I don't know what got into him, but I'll take care of it later."

As dinner ended and just as everybody was ready to scatter to the four winds, the dad said, "Wait a minute. Everybody sit back down." He reached under the table and brought up a tape recorder, and said, "I secretly taped tonight's dinner conversation. We all say goofy things around the table, and to prove how nutty we all are and how much fun we have, I'm going to rewind the tape, and let's listen to some of our chatter." They all laughed and settled back in their chairs to hear the tape. Mom and Dad were talking about their important adult day, the two teens were bragging about what was important to them, when all of a sudden a little boy voice, barely audible, said, "Will someone please pass me the potatoes?" The other four continued their nonstop talking over each other's chatter when again, a bit louder, "Will someone please pass me the potatoes?" Talk, talk, talk, chatter, chatter, chatter, and then the infamous "Pass those potatoes!"

Dad turned off the tape and said, "Whoops—we blew it."

The oldest son said, "Yeah, we think we're so important. We forget he's as important as we are—and just as important to God." The family then trotted down the hall to apologize to the boy. He was a happy camper that night as he got not one but *two* desserts, but he also agreed not to do his Tarzan yell in the future. The family promised to show interest to each other on an equal basis.

2. *Mind Wandering*

We can listen several times faster than the person we're listening to can speak. That gives us a lot of time for our mind to switch to other thoughts. But that can prove to be embarrassing when the person talking to us asks us for a response to what was just said. Since we were "floating," we haven't heard their last five sentences. At times we're also busy preparing our rebuttal so we aren't focusing on what the other person is saying. Pretty sad communicating, isn't it? Prov. 29:20 says, "Do you see a man who speaks in haste? There is more hope for a fool than for him."

3. *Fixing*

One of the biggest problems with couples is when one of them wants to fix a problem that the other doesn't want fixed. The latter person just wants to be listened to.

"Honey, tell me how you feel. I'll try to understand."

"It sounds so dumb."

"No, it won't. Tell me what's making you so unhappy?"

"Oh, nothing really."

"Come on, Honey. What is it?"

"I just feel like a failure because I was passed over for the promotion."

"I can't believe that. You aren't a failure because of it. You know the other guy has more training and experience than you, and he was first in line for the job. So don't feel that way. You'll get another opportunity. You have to think positively."

Good intentions, yet why is it we want to "fix it" with our good advice before we have really heard what the other person is trying to say? So often we jump in before the person has a chance to fully express himself or herself. We prematurely judge and criticize each other and then wonder why our mate or kids don't want to talk to us.

In reading the above, if you saw yourself doing those things, there's still hope. It's not too late. Listening is something we all can learn, so we're going to look at three listening keys that will help us better understand what is going on inside the other person's world.

Key No. 1—Listen with Your Heart

Listening with your heart means you're listening to the feelings behind the words being expressed to you. Try to listen and understand from the other person's perspective.

It's like the little girl who was sent on an errand by her mother. She was gone longer than she should have been. When she arrived home the mother wanted an explanation, so the little girl said, "I met Mary on the way and her doll was broken, so I stopped to help her."

The mother said, "Oh, that's nice. You fixed her doll for her?"

The little girl replied, "No, I stopped to cry with her."

She didn't go into the fixing mode but took the time to empathize. Empathy is not sympathy, which is feeling sorry for someone. Rather, it's seeing the world from that person's viewpoint, feeling what he or she feels. That's what's spoken about in Rom. 12:15: "Rejoice with those who rejoice; mourn with those who mourn." It's not always easy, but it really begins with our having an attitude that what my mate is saying is important, and I'm going to try to understand.

Key No. 2—Listen with Your Ears

In other words, tune in. We heard a story that former President Franklin Roosevelt once said that nobody inside Washington, D.C., listens to anyone. He said that everybody is so preoccupied trying to climb the political and social ladders that they don't really tune people in. To prove his point to one of his aides, at the next White House reception as he was greeting everyone coming through the reception line, he leaned forward and said to them, "This morning I murdered my grandmother." Not one person paid any attention to what the president of the United States just said to him or her. Easing along the reception line, getting closer to the president, each was in his or her own private world, repeating some little memorized line to say to the president and glancing into the main ballroom to see what important senator or military leader might be there. Suddenly each person was aware that the president said something, so he or she extended his or her hand, mumbled his or her memorized line, and scampered into the ballroom to ricochet around the political and social contacts.

Well, let's correct that. *One* person actually heard the president—a diplomat from a third-world country. When the president said, "This morning I murdered my grandmother," the diplomat stepped forward, clasped both of Roosevelt's hands, and quietly said, "Mr. President, I'm sure she had it coming to her." That man was the only person to tune in.

Are you having a hard time tuning in? If you really want to be an effective listener, the major distractions are what we call "the three Ts": television, telephone, and tiredness. Whatever those distractions are in your life, get rid of them.

Remember when Tiger Woods blew away the course in the U.S. Open not long ago? Remember how he and his father hugged when it was over and sobbed tears of joy together? That was a very touching father-and-son moment. But it actually started years before. In an interview, Tiger's dad said, "Whatever age Tiger was, when he wanted to talk with me, I always put down my paper or turned off the TV and we talked. That has always been the case since he was an infant, and that's the case still today." Tiger knew his father valued him.

Listening with our ears also means "Don't interrupt." Prov. 18:13 says, "He who answers before listening—that is his folly and his shame." Both of us have a tendency to interrupt each other. We've both had to learn to control our tongues and show courtesy so the other could finish his or her sentence—otherwise we'd never understand what each other is saying. We have also learned not to finish each other's sentences. We saw a cartoon in which a woman was peeling a potato in her kitchen. Her husband was sitting next to her and said, "Sugar, I think . . ." but before he could finish his sentence, she interrupted and said, ". . . like a pig." She concluded by saying, "Whoops. There I go again. Finishing your sentences." Be careful. The longer you're married, the easier it is to slip into this pattern. When that happens, remember that at that point you're just listening to words and not understanding what the other person is trying to get across.

Key No. 3—Listen with Your Eyes

Watch the person you're listening to, because his or her *body* is also talking. And it speaks loudly. Have you ever tried to communicate something to your mate, but you didn't want to use words, so you indicated instead with your eyes or another part of your body?

Yvonne: *When we were first married we were having dinner at the home of some of Bob's longtime friends. As a young bride I was nervous meeting a number of his old friends and wanted to leave a good impression. We were seated across from each other at the table, and during the dinner Bob made a remark about me that I didn't appreciate. I wanted to get his attention and show him I didn't like it, but he didn't seem to look at me. So I decided to give him a swift kick under the table, hoping that would bring his eyes around so I could give him "the look."*

Now, I knew that technique worked in the movies, but it sure didn't for me. When he felt the kick, he quickly turned to me and said very loudly, "Ouch! Why did you kick me?" As all eyes turned toward me, all I can say is that my face turned a bright Hawaiian sunset red, and I wanted to crawl under the table. Since then I have learned a swift kick doesn't work to get his attention. I need to use another nonverbal sign.

Communication is much more than just words. Many years ago the Kodak Corporation conducted a study and discovered that 7 percent of what we mean when we communicate comes through our words, 38 percent comes through our tone of voice, and 55 percent comes through our body language—our nonverbal communication. The latter is our facial expressions, posture, hand gestures, and so on. All of that sends a message. That's why you need to look when you listen.

Let's say you have a young son coming home after school. He enters the house, drops his bag with a large thud, and slams the door. You ask him how his day was, and he responds with "Fine." But his tone sounds dejected, and as you glance at him you notice his shoulders are slumped and his eyes are downcast. You can tell that his words don't go along with the message his body is showing. Now if you just listened to his words, you would never pursue any further to find out what's really going on inside of him. But by listening with your eyes you will see something isn't jelling with him, and that's when you go over to him and gently say, "Come on—what's going on? I want to listen." A message is received correctly if the words match the tone of voice and the nonverbal indicators. A message is not received correctly if the words differ from the other two. The listener will believe the actions instead of the words.

The SOLER Method

An effective method we've used to help us listen better is called the "SOLER" method. It goes like this:

S—Squarely face the person. You want to directly face the person, not give him or her a partial shoulder.

O—Open up your body. By opening up your body you make the person relaxed. Unfold your arms and relax your hands.

L—Lean in. If you don't quite catch a word, say, "Please repeat that," and lean in just a smidgen. That shows the person that you care, that you think he or she is important, and that you want to hear what he or she is saying.

E—Eye contact. If you look at other people or other things while listening, the other person will get the impression you don't care.

R—Respond. When someone has said something to you, respond back to what he or she has said.

Let's expand on this one a little more. Example: A husband and wife are taking a walk around their neighborhood. She says, "It's such a beautiful day. I can't believe the rain they're predicting will be here tonight." His response is silence. She wonders what's going on with him since he didn't respond. Often the silence is taken in a negative fashion, as if something is wrong.

Let's redo that conversation. She says, "It's such a beautiful day. I can't believe the rain they're predicting will be here tonight."

His response is, "That's right. It *is* hard to believe, but that's what they're predicting."

She says, "I'll bet you two big kisses that they're wrong on their predictions."

He laughs and says, "You're on." This is part of having a conversation with each other. To run a continual monologue is not satisfying in the communication process. It needs to go back and forth.

Another way to respond is to reflect back what is being said. Don't be a parrot and just repeat it word for word, but instead, paraphrase what you're hearing:

"I don't know how to handle this rather unusual problem with John."

"He's doing something that upsets you?"

"Well, don't laugh, but he never says no. I ask him for a favor and I know at times it's an imposition, but he won't say no."

"He seems to have difficulty refusing you?"

"Yes, I wonder what I do that causes him not to say no."

"You think it's something you do?"

"Yes. Maybe I should talk to him."

Responding in this manner makes the person feel understood.

The manner in which you communicate can convey the love of Jesus Christ in a very practical way. That's why it's important to become a positive communicator.

Commit to a Time to Talk

We suggest that you make a commitment to communicate. Sure—at times it's easier to say, "Ah, forget it" and walk away or get frustrated with the process and shut down. But your relationship will suffer, and you won't be able to maintain your team spirit. We encourage you for the rest of your married life to be committed to communicate, and an important key to this commitment is taking the time to communicate with your spouse.

Many years ago we read Alan Loy McGinnis's book *The Friendship Factor* in which he writes about an experiment a psychologist conducted that would measure the amount of conversation that occurs weekly between an average husband and wife. To make sure the experiment was accurate, the researcher strapped portable electronic microphones onto the subjects. They then measured every word the couple uttered, which included everything from idle conversations that occurred while in the car driving with their mate to requests to pass the salt at the dinner table.

There are 10,080 minutes in a week. How much time do you suppose the average couple devotes to talking to each other in a week's time, according to the study? Not 10 hours. Not a single hour. Not even 30 minutes. They averaged a grand total of *17 minutes.*[1] And couples think they can build a lasting marriage on 17 minutes a week? No way! No wonder so many spouses don't feel a closeness with their mate. They aren't spending much time discovering each other through communication.

Spending high-quality time together was a major problem for us. Since we live together, work together, and travel together, you would think we have plenty of time to talk with each other. Granted, we were able to grab snatches of time to discuss an upcoming speaking engagement or a business decision we had to make. We thought we talked a lot with each other, so we couldn't understand why we were feeling such a distance in our relationship. Besides the distance, we found a tension between us, and we started bickering a lot. Then the realization hit us that our conversations always centered around work, and we weren't spending any time just enjoying each other's company through conversation. We were missing out on sharing our thoughts and ideas with each other. We were especially missing out on any growth time together, because we never had time for it. That realization alerted us that we needed to make a change.

We want to share with you the four communication times we installed in our marriage that made a big difference. Maybe they can help you also.

Daily Talk Times

Each day we have 30-plus minutes put aside for top-quality talk time. For us it's our dinnertime. Mealtime has always been important conversation time for our family. When our son was living at home, that was our family connection time. We would find out about each other's day as well as talk about mutual subjects of interest. Unfortunately, for years that was the only time we had to talk together. We should have put in some extra time for just us, but we didn't. Now since our son is married and it's just the two of us at home, our main talk time is again around the dinner table. We decided that this was not going to be just a time to talk about those dreaded bills, upcoming appointments, or discussions about our work and ministry, but it would mainly be a time to learn something new about each other. We would ask each other creative questions (see examples at the end of the chapter). Plus we'd talk about current events, biblical prophecy, politics, and so on.

Having this designated talk time on a regular basis has changed one thing that used to happen frequently. For instance, if Bob were standing in front of Yvonne and he didn't have that glazed-over look, Yvonne would think, "He's possibly listening to me," so she'd unload everything she had been storing up for weeks. Yvonne felt she never knew when she would get his attention again, so she didn't want to pass up this golden opportunity. When the barrage occurred, Bob would dive for cover. It was an overload. Now this daily talk time has taken off that pressure.

About now you may be asking, "But what about the little grievances that come up daily—such as my mate being late again, or the clothes that aren't picked up, or a decision about which summer camp the kids should attend this year. Stuff like that. When do you talk about them?"

Common sense guides us. If it's something that needs to be addressed immediately, we do it on the spot. If it can wait until our daily talk time, we bring it up then. But we've agreed to not spend all of our talk time on grievances. And if it's something that can wait for a few days or will take some time to solve, we'll wait for our next talk time—the weekly one.

Weekly Talk Times

Our weekly talk time is a special time when we get out of our house and go to a local eatery so we can give each other our undivided attention and spend from one to two hours together. We discuss any grievances that could wait until this time, problem-solve, and go over our schedule for the next couple of weeks to make sure we're on the same track about our family life and business life. Leading such busy lives, we find this weekly time helps keep us in balance. If you have small children, maybe a neighbor could watch them for an hour or two while you head off for your weekly time. We know one couple who couldn't get away for that time period, so they set aside Saturday mornings as their time. They would get up, feed the kids, put on a children's videotape, and hang a "Do not disturb" sign on their bedroom door. They would have their breakfast in their room and spend at least an hour talking. Their kids were all for it and even reminded Mom and Dad if they failed to do it some Saturday morning. Find out what works for you.

Hanging-Around Times

Have you discovered, like us, that some of your best conversations are not planned but happen spontaneously? We've discovered this with children, especially when they're teenagers. Hanging around them, we've experienced many good chats as they bring up a myriad of subjects. They do so more readily in a casual atmosphere. Yvonne remembers those hanging-around times with her dad. When she was little, whenever her dad was taking the trash to the town dump, he would ask if she wanted to go along. She would pile into the car, excited to see the treasures people threw away at the dump.

Yvonne: *I guess the beginning of my love for bargain hunting started at the town dump. But more than that, it was a time to spend talking with my dad. On the way home we always stopped at the local coffee shop for a piece of pie. As we sat at the counter I always felt like such an adult, and we would just enjoy the moment and talk. That was a wonderful pattern my dad set early in my life. As you can readily tell, having him hang out and talk with me is something I'll never forget. Now as an adult when I go see Dad, we no longer head for the dump, but I'll go with him as he runs to the hardware store, and then we'll stop off for something to eat, and we talk. Over the years through our talk time my dad and I have continued a relationship that hasn't been broken.*

It's the same way in your marriage. It's those times you make to just hang out with each other that may illicit some wonderful conversations. It's often those small blocks of time when you share your thoughts and heart with each other. For us, some of our best hanging-out times occur between April and November. That's when our outdoor community pool is open. We take a break from work midmorning, Monday through Friday. That's when people are usually in school or at work. Even during the summer months kids usually don't hit the water until the afternoon, so we have it almost entirely to ourselves. We swim, talk, and play. Sometimes it's just playful talk. Other times it's been deeply meaningful. For Bob it's a very relaxing time, and he tends to open up more while in the pool. We walk back home renewed and refreshed.

Going for a walk in our neighborhood is another special time for us to connect, plus it's a good way to stay in shape. You don't have to do the same things we do, but find something that works for you.

Escape Times

Escape times for us are when we get alone for a date or romantic interlude right in our own home, an overnight stay at a nearby beach hotel, or sometimes even a weekender.

Yvonne: *When we first started these escape times, I had such high expectations that we would spend all our time having deep, meaningful conversations. I found out that those deep conversations didn't always happen, and then I would be disappointed. I've now changed my thinking since we started having more opportunities to talk. I now just go with the flow wherever we are. I've learned to enjoy just being in my husband's presence, and if a deep conversation comes out of it, it's an added treat.*

Keep in mind these escape times don't just happen. You have to make them happen. To do this, you have to practice the three "P's" that Linda Dillow speaks about in her book *How to Really Love Your Man*—pray, plan, and persevere.[2]

Pray

Your Heavenly Father is concerned about every detail of your life. Deut. 4:7 says, "The LORD our God is near us whenever we pray to him." Pray for those times to talk and be alone. God will help you rearrange schedules, open doors as to who will look after your children, and give you creative ideas for your escape times.

Plan

Why bother planning? Have you noticed how life has a way of filling up with so many "things"? Pressures from others come, so we tend to put our marriage and our times together on the back burner. Last year we talked about going to a particular event we were both interested in. At first we were traveling, but we agreed to go later. Then we would say, "We're kind of busy today. Let's go tomorrow." Before we knew it, the event was over and it was impossible to go. We learned from that experience. We now plan times together as well as guard those times.

Persevere

At times it will feel as though everything and everyone is against your having time together as a couple.

Yvonne: *I remember one Valentine's Day that I had planned for the two of us. We were going to stay home (since we travel all the time, one of our biggest thrills is to stay at home). I had a special night set up with a candlelight bubble bath, sparkling apple cider, our favorite truffles, romantic talk, and, well, you can imagine it from there. We both anticipated that night for a whole week. We would make mention of it during the days leading up to it plus leave each other love notes around the house telling each other how much we were looking forward to that special night. Get the picture?*

But that night didn't arrive as anticipated. On Valentine's Day morning Bob got hit with the flu—a bad case. We're both very health-conscious, so for either one of us to get sick is rare and a surprise. Yes, we were disappointed, but it didn't stop us from having our special night—five days later. We could have given up, but we decided it was important to us, so we persevered.

Getting those times together isn't always easy. That's why you need to pray, plan, and persevere. It's well worth the effort.

We close this chapter with Ps. 19:14: "May the words of my mouth and the meditation of my heart be pleasing in your sight, O LORD, my Rock and my Redeemer."

TEAM-BUILDING QUESTIONS

1. Consider whether you've been more of a negative communicator or a positive communicator. Why do you think so? (You may want to refer back to the barriers to showing appreciation, described in this chapter.)
2. Do you experience any of the barriers to listening? Decide on a plan of action to overcome those barriers.

3. How well do you listen? Together fill out your responses to the following. Circle the answer that best describes your communication pattern for each question.

1. Do you find yourself distracted by television, housework, or other activities when your spouse attempts to talk with you?

always   often   seldom   never

2. When your spouse is talking, are you already thinking about your response?

always   often   seldom   never

3. Do you allow time in your busy schedule to listen to your spouse?

always   often   seldom   never

4. Does your spouse ever accuse you of not listening or understanding?

always   often   seldom   never

5. Do you listen without interrupting?

always   often   seldom   never

6. Are you a good listener when someone outside your family needs to talk to you?

always   often   seldom   never

7. Do you reflect or restate what you've heard to see if you understand what your spouse has said?

always   often   seldom   never

Take time to discuss these questions and answers. Ask your mate to pick just one of the questions to which you answered "always." That's where you can begin to work on your communication skills.

TEAM-BUILDING ACTION STEPS

1. Decide on a daily and weekly time and place in which you and your spouse can have some uninterrupted time together.
2. "Talk Time Questions." Incorporate one a week into your talk times to expand your knowledge of each other. This is a discovery time, not a time to correct or evaluate what your spouse is expressing.
   - What was your favorite day ever and why?
   - What is your most cherished gift ever received?
   - Who is your favorite relative? Why?
   - What modern invention do you believe we would be better off without?
   - If you had a thousand dollars, how would you spend it tomorrow?

- If you had free use of a billboard for two weeks, what message would you put on it?
- What famous living person would you like to spend a day with?
- If women were required by law to have a beard or be bald, which would you choose?
- What color other than black and white should asphalt be?
- What was your favorite toy as a child?
- What one truth do you wish someone had told you before marriage?
- If you could choose anyone as your mentor for the next two years, who would it be?
- At what great historical event would you like to have been present?

Father, through my communication to my mate,
help me plant flowers instead of weeds.

9

Making Conflict Work for You

TEAM BUILDING THROUGH PROBLEM SOLVING

The goal in marriage is not to think alike,
but to think together.
—Robert C. Dodds

*C*an anything *positive* come out of a conflict?" We hear that question quite often in our ministry. Usually conflict is thought to be an indication that there must be something really wrong with the relationship, that the marriage must be in the pits. But we need to realize that since we're individuals, some conflict is as inevitable as a daily sunrise.

Many circumstances produce conflict. See if you can relate to any of the following:

1. Spouse 1: "But, Honey, we're *lost*. Why can't we stop and ask for directions?"
   Spouse 2: "Don't need to. I'll find it."
   (Male and female differences.)

2. Spouse 1: "But our family has always opened our gifts on Christmas *Eve,* not Christmas Day."
   Spouse 2: "Well, sorry—our family always did it the *right* way—Christmas morning."
   (Background differences.)

3. Spouse 1: "You're supposed to because . . ."
   Spouse 2: "Yeah? Well, I just assumed . . ."
   (Expectations and assumptions.)

159

4. Unexpectedly an amount of money comes your way.
   Spouse 1: "I want to sock this away in our savings account."
   Spouse 2: "We can save money when the next windfall hits
      us, but right now we desperately need some new furni-
      ture." (Priority differences.)
5. "Why, after taking things out of the cupboard, can't you put
   them back instead of leaving them all over the house?" (Personality differences.)
6. Choose your conflict-producer: stress, fatigue, financial
   strains, raising children, in-law problems.
7. Or choose from this list: sin, selfishness, irresponsibility.
8. And don't forget—your mate knows what *hot* button to push
   to get you to become a member of the Wall-climbers' Club.
   Such as "I can't believe you did that again. That's unbeliev-
   able."

We've had disagreements about where to spend our vacations (and how long—Bob prefers short; Yvonne prefers long),
what time to arrive at church (Bob prefers 10 to 15 minutes before the start; Yvonne prefers a minute before the opening
hymn), how to deal with money (doesn't everybody?), and
even how to coordinate writing this book. We also admit that
we have some *serious* conflicts in our household—over such
things as which direction the toilet paper should roll, what the
temperature should be in the car on a long trip, and how to
squeeze our shared tube of toothpaste (one of us is a precise
squeezer, from the bottom to the top, while the other takes a
creative squeeze-it-wherever approach). As we said, *very serious*
conflicts.

But really, as you can see, conflict can and does enter into
every couple's relationship. Some people believe that "good"
marriages should not have conflict. Some go as far as to say,
"Why, we've never had a fight." That usually means their conflicts are not out in the open but hidden under the table. Their
differences mostly go unresolved. When they don't have a way
to work out their differences, their marriage can end up lacking
any kind of warmth or spark. Instead, they've erected many invisible walls of resentment between them. How sad and unnec-
essary that is!

We have discovered that conflict isn't something to be
afraid of. You can walk arm in arm without seeing eye to eye.

And we have learned that properly handled conflict can be used to strengthen your marriage team. How? It can help your relationship grow as it teaches you many things about yourself. It will show you areas you may need to change that you wouldn't have seen without the conflict. When you have a way to resolve your problems, you'll realize that your love can withstand trials and disagreements, and through your problem solving you will have stronger security in your marriage.

Good News, Bad News

Stronger security in your marriage—that's the good news. The bad news is that conflict handled improperly can lead to combat. Continued combat can lead to what Mark 3:25 speaks about: "If a house is divided against itself, that house cannot stand." If conflict cannot be resolved, communication breaks down further until the marriage gets stuck. Instead of working with each other, couples wind up working against each other.

But there's another problem that we often overlook. Warring parents greatly affect their children. If you are a warring parent, your kids will start to believe that your problems are their fault. This causes them to feel insecure as they start to fret that Mom and Dad will get a divorce. Warring parents cause their offspring to live in fear. If you are a parent, surely that's not your intent.

Knowing there's going to be conflict in your marriage and handling it effectively are two different ball games—especially when most of us have learned to *mis*manage conflict. A large part of the way you handle conflict comes from the way you were raised, but it also comes from "on-the-job training" as a new spouse when you learn to deal with problems within your marriage. Here are four ways that we've *mis*managed conflict.

The Dove (I want peace at any price)[1]

The dove is aware there's a conflict but chooses not to deal with it or else procrastinates in hopes that the problem will just go away. The dove's method of operation is nonengagement. In order to keep peace, no matter what, the dove constantly gives in to his or her mate. He or she will say, "OK—I guess we'll do it your way," "No, no—it's my fault," or "Sure—I'll do whatever you want. No need to get mad."

The biblical story of Samson and Delilah is an ancient classic example. The original Mr. Hulk yielded to her demands. Result? He wound up being a blinded slave and met a crushing death—literally.

Even though a dove won't deal with conflict, he or she will let you know something is wrong. How? By putting distance between you, such as pouting and giving the silent treatment. We know a couple with whom conflict occurs daily, but the wife won't talk to her husband. He prods her to resolve the conflict but usually gives up. Nothing gets resolved. She retreats because early in the marriage, when she would bring things up to her husband, he would always strive to win and win handily. He hurt her so much that she decided the only way to deal with their conflicts was to go the dove route—withdraw.

The Hawk (It's your fault)

Picture a person with the conflict personality of a hawk. Arms folded in front, steely jaw set, feet firmly planted, saying, "We're going to do it *my* way."

A hawk likes to force its way on others, but in a marriage all of this is done at the expense of the mate.

A hawk sets out to win and enjoys keeping score by changing the topic, such as, "Yes, but what about when you . . ." The mate of a hawk feels continual competition, and he or she always ends up a loser. Since the hawk's method of operation is *attack,* he or she may win battles but inevitably loses the war as the marriage suffers.

This can occur especially when both husband and wife play the hawk role. They are locked in a perpetual power struggle. An example: Jules and Michele. Michele told us, "I've built up a protective shell around me that I'm afraid to let Jules penetrate. I've always been competitive, and so has Jules, so it feels that we're competing to win all the time. We both have a lot of ammunition stored up to use at the right moments. I sometimes would let my shell down to get things settled, but if I did, Jules may take advantage of me, go for the kill, and then I'd lose."

Actually they would both lose because they're a team. On a

team you can't have a winner and a loser. Either the whole team wins or it loses.

The Owl (Let's be reasonable)

The method of operation for the owl is manipulation. Often the manipulation is subtle, but the object is to get the spouse to do what he or she wants. The owl uses blame to shift the focus to his or her mate. This tactic is hardly new. It originated with Adam and Eve in the garden over the conflict of eating the fruit from the tree of knowledge. Adam launched the first owl missile when he said, "God, it's because of the woman *you* gave me that I did it." Eve countered with, "I ate the fruit, but it wasn't my fault. It was because of the serpent. He made me do it."

Owls are also very good at making you feel guilty—really guilty. An owl husband could say to his wife, "Darling, I would spend more time with you, but I only wanted to please you when I bought this large, expensive house, so I have to work long hours six days a week to pay for it." Ouch.

So "Darling" feels guilty and decides she's probably asking too much of him. Later that day, when he does have some time off, he decides to go golfing. She realizes that once again he has turned the tables on her. A person married to an owl feels controlled, so neither spouse works together toward a solution to the problem.

The Ostrich (Conflict? What conflict?)

The method of operation for the ostrich is denial. An ostrich believes that conflict is destructive to a relationship, so it's better to deny that any conflict is occurring. The reasoning is "If ignored, the conflict will go away."

Jonah of the Old Testament is an example of this. He had an inner conflict with what God had told him to do—go to Nineveh and tell the people of their coming destruction. Jonah wasn't too thrilled to share such unhappy news with these folks, so he decided to ignore the request and run from it. As you know, his Olympic swimming style was terrible, and he was swallowed up by a great fish that finally threw him up on the shores of Nineveh, the last place he wanted to be. He tried to deny the actuality of all this, but God wanted him to face this inner conflict.

Has there been a conflict you've been denying, one that God wants you to confront?

One man told us that he had been married more than 40 years and that his secret to a long-term marriage was "When we were first married I decided that any time we were starting an argument, I would simply go out for a long walk. Seems that in these 40 years I have spent more time outdoors than indoors, and I'm in great shape." Yes, he said that with a twinkle in his eye, but our point is that denying that conflict exists does not make the problem disappear. It will *always* be under the surface, ready to rear its head at any time.

Do you see yourself in any of these styles? Unfortunately, with these four ways of *mis*managing conflict, the result is couples who feel estranged from each other.

Something else that can make you feel estranged from your spouse is the *way* you handle anger.

Dealing with Your Anger

Where there is conflict there is usually anger. One of the biggest problems in marriage is not knowing how to handle anger. Anger in itself doesn't hurt relationships. It's the way we choose to express anger that can be a problem. Like leveling an anthill with a 20-ton bulldozer, or pruning a rosebush with a turbo-powered chainsaw.

Occasionally at some of our seminars when we mention the topic of dealing with one's anger, there are some folks who shrug it off and say in so many words, "Oh, that's no big deal." But if it's not dealt with correctly, it can divide your marriage.

Couples often find themselves caught up in a cycle of angry words. One spouse starts with words that convey a message of attack on his or her mate: "I'm so angry because you never take me out anymore" or "You don't care about me, because all you do is think about your old selfish self."

Your mate will automatically get defensive, because your remarks produce feelings of inadequacy and judgment. Then comes the counterattack: "I don't take you out anymore because all you ever do is complain. It's bad enough that I have to listen to your complaining at home; why should I suffer in public too?" You launch another zinger, and it's fended off and countered with another retort. The verbal Ping-Pong match goes on with the two of you accusing each other until one finally gives up and stomps off.

Instead of dealing with the problem behind the emotions and settling it, the event leaves everybody frustrated and hurt, and nothing is solved. This pattern is repeated several times, and before long it's hard to feel "warm fuzzies" toward your mate. Many just isolate themselves instead of opting to work as a team.

Many circumstances occur in our lives that bring on anger. We were created in God's image to experience a wide range of emotions. Anger is one of them, and God's anger is recorded more than 300 times in the Old Testament. That's right—more than 300 times it is written that *God got angry.* Jesus was also like us in that He, too, had the emotion of anger. He experienced anger such as when the Pharisees criticized Him for healing a man on the Sabbath, or when He saw men exchanging money in the house of the Lord. He expressed anger, yes, but it was always directed at the action, not the person, so Jesus did not sin.

In our marriage we want our anger to be a positive force that can be used by God to bring about changes in our relationship. In allowing God to direct all that energy, we're expanding into a positive problem-solving mode.

The Bible speaks clearly about anger. In Eph. 4:26 Paul writes, "In your anger do not sin." Wow—how can we possibly do what that verse says? For this to occur, we need to better understand what anger really is.

First of all, anger is not a behavior but an emotion. We want to repeat that—*anger is not a behavior but an emotion.* It is a *secondary* emotion. Another emotion brought it on, and it happens so fast that often we're not even aware of that. Our feelings of anger go through a quick two-step process.

Step 1—Emotions Are Aroused

Something happens in your life. It could be a negative action taken toward you or negative words spoken to you. Your initial reaction is an arousal emotion, which usually is one of the following four other emotions:

    A. Fear—such as feeling out of control, ignored, rejected, or ridiculed.

B. Hurt—which comes from not feeling appreciated or your mate forgetting something that's important to you.

C. Frustration—when things are not going according to your plans; when life doesn't seem fair.

D. Disappointment—with something you looked forward to or thought would happen, and it didn't.

These emotions then produce the second step.

Step 2 — Thoughts Are Triggered

Thoughts are then triggered, which we usually say silently to ourselves. They are triggered by the arousal emotion. They come in the thought forms of what we call the "shoulds" and the "blamers."

They sound like this: "He should understand me," "She shouldn't treat me this way," "Why didn't you . . . ?" "What? You've got to be kidding. *You're* the one who made me do it!" "No way. It's not my fault. It's *your* fault. Look at what you've done." Or how about this one? "Couldn't you just once . . . ?" If you add these trigger thoughts onto the arousal emotion, guess what's next? Out comes anger. That's why we call anger a secondary emotion.

Let's see how this all plays out from an experience Yvonne recently had as she was driving down an on-ramp to merge on-to the freeway.

Yvonne: *As I was driving down the on-ramp, I was judging where I was going to fit in the stream of cars that was in the slow lane. As I started to merge, a car obviously sped up so there was no room for me to enter. In most cases this would be OK as I would have the shoulder of the freeway to still drive on. The problem in this case was there was road construction and the shoulder was blocked off with a concrete wall. I was heading for the wall at high speed. I had to suddenly slam on my brakes and swerve to get behind another car. I was not a bit pleased with what happened, and I was instantly angry with the other driver.*

As Yvonne examined this experience, utilizing the two-step model, she found that the primary emotion she felt was fear—fear that she would slam into the wall. Then the trigger thoughts came: "This isn't fair. I play by the rules; that driver should too. What a thoughtless person!" Then the anger came out.

You may be thinking, "That's interesting, but what does that have to do with making sure I don't sin when I'm angry?"

Remember that we said anger is an emotion, not a behavior. When you're angry, you have a choice as to the behavior you will exhibit. This is where most of us get into trouble, especially in our marriage, and if it's not handled correctly, we slip into sin. Yvonne's story continues.

Yvonne: *When my anger sprang up, I had a choice as to what to do with the anger. I could go into a Lady Rambo revenge mode and go after that driver, wishing I had a bazooka in my car, which would not be pleasing to God and could get me into major trouble. Or I could give that driver the benefit of the doubt and assume that he or she was simply not paying close attention to merging traffic and didn't intentionally speed up, so I chose to let the incident go.*

It's not the anger itself that gets us into trouble; it's the behavior we choose due to the anger. The two ways that get us into trouble and cause us to slip into sin are either (1) we blow up or (2) we clam up.

Blow Up

If your motivation is to seek vengeance, then you'll want to hurt the person as he or she has hurt you. One way is to become verbally abusive with name-calling, yelling, or threats. Or you do something physical such as slam doors, drive crazily, or hit. None of these responses are an effective way to deal with anger—especially the ones dealing with hitting and threats. Actions like those, if not addressed early on, can lead to more serious behaviors and consequences.

Some people are under the false assumption that "I can lower my anger by blowing up and just getting it out of my system." Wrong. All that does is set up an endless cycle in marriage in which you blow up, your mate's defenses go up, your mate blows up, you blow up all the more, and the lose-lose cycle continues. Prov. 30:33 says, "Stirring up anger produces strife." And in 29:11 we're warned, "A fool gives full vent to his anger." Don't be considered a fool.

Clam Up

You end up suffering in many ways when you clam up. Physically your body can feel the results, from ulcers to arthritis. Your emotions are affected and you might suffer from depression because your anger went inward. Spiritually you feel separated from God, because with the hurt you push God away. Relationally, when you're holding a grudge and your desire is vengeance, it pushes others away. God has a better way for us to deal with anger so that we don't sin. And that is to—

Speak Up

By speaking up you're expressing your thoughts and feelings, but you must do so without attacking your mate. We have found that to express our thoughts, we both need a cooling-off period to get our anger under control so we can be "quick to listen, slow to speak and slow to become angry" (James 1:19). We did that so we wouldn't say anything that we would later regret.

Bob: *I would walk away for a while so I could think this over and figure out how to solve it, but I neglected to tell Yvonne that that's what I needed to do.*

Yvonne: *I interpreted it as his escaping from the problem, so I went right after him like a clucking mother hen after her brood. I wanted to talk it out right then and on the spot. It only heightened our problem, and nothing was resolved.*

We have since learned that we both benefit from a cooling-off period. During this time we both put on our thinking caps and start praying to the Lord, asking Him to reveal why we are pitted against each other. At times Yvonne has found that writing her thoughts down on paper helps her sift through them. She'll then give them to Bob to read.

After the cooling-off period we're ready to speak up, always keeping in mind Eph. 4:15, "Speaking the truth in love." Often our problem isn't that we don't speak the truth but that we don't speak the truth in love. We've found the best way to express our thoughts, feelings, and ideas is to use what we call "I" messages. These are sentences that express how we're feeling or reacting to what just happened. We prefer those to "you" messages in which we're telling each other how the other person needs to change in order to please me. A "you" message could be like this: "You're supposed to be a Christian, so how can you stand there and say such things?" Naturally, the other one feels attacked, so the arguing intensifies.

Instead, an "I" message tells how the other's words affected you, like "I feel hurt and angry when I'm criticized for what I cook for dinner, because I try to cook what you would like."

This is living out Prov. 15:1: "A gentle answer turns away wrath, but a harsh word stirs up anger."

Speaking up in this manner will keep the communication bridge open so you can work toward solving the problem. We've looked at dealing with anger so it doesn't slip into sin, but look at the latter part of Eph. 4:26, where Paul writes, "Do not let the sun go down while you are still angry." Now that's practical. How well do *you* sleep if you both go to bed angry?

For some couples, getting ready for bed is something that qualifies to be seen on *America's Funniest Home Videos*. Example: The husband and wife aren't talking to each other and pass in the house like the other one isn't even part of Planet Earth. They close down the house for bedtime, and the wife thinks, "That man is *not* going to see my body tonight." So she goes into the bathroom, slams the door, puts on three nightgowns and her steel-belted bathrobe, grabs a can of mace in one hand and the panic alarm button in the other hand, and stomps off to bed. As they enter their king-sized bed, one spouse balances on the edge of the side of the bed facing away, while the other balances on the opposite rim of the "Grand Canyon," as far away from the other as possible.

The wife thinks, "If ol' Buffalo Brains would just admit he's wrong and apologize, then we could both get some sleep." But unfortunately, the lord of the castle is now fast asleep and snoring louder than thunder.

She can't let *him* sleep while *she's* wide awake, so she leaps out of bed, stomps into the bathroom, and starts slamming the toilet seat up and down. She makes more noise and commotion than an amusement park ride. She's thinking, "If *I'm* not sleeping, then *he's* not sleeping." The sudden loud noise startles him, and he roars out of bed with eyes wider than a night owl but growls like a bear, "Hey—what's going on?" Really mature, isn't it? Well, though a bit exaggerated, that was sort of like us for many years.

We have since learned that we may not settle the whole conflict near bedtime, but at least we know to deal with the anger before we go to sleep. Why? To refuse giving the devil a foothold in our marriage (Eph. 4:27).

The devil doesn't need much to get you two separated and not working together as a team. Not dealing with your anger starts out with a small crack, and if it isn't dealt with, it becomes a large fissure with the two of you standing on opposite sides—arms crossed, frowns on your faces—waiting for the other to become humble and make the first move. The evil one now has you competing rather than completing each other.

This foothold can work negatively on your children. The way you deal with anger influences them. Anger is learned. Just as you learned how to deal with it from your parents, you are passing the same to your kids. Prov. 22:24-25 speaks to this: "Do not make friends with a hot-tempered man, do not associate with one easily angered, or you may learn his ways and get yourself ensnared." But as a parent you can break the generational cycle with learning to deal with anger by speaking up.

Now that you have dealt with your anger, you will be more open to deal with the actual problem and try to work (hopefully) as a team to find the solution. We have developed a seven-step plan for resolving conflict that has proven effective for our relationship. We're confident it will do the same for you.

Step 1— Schedule a Peace Talk

In most cases your conflict does not have to be dealt with immediately. As long as the anger has been dealt with, the conflict can be settled at another time. Here are a couple of guidelines for your peace talk.

Choose the Right Time

An old adage warns, "Never discuss a problem standing up or on an empty stomach." Choose a time when both of you will be receptive to listening to each other, but make sure it's within 48 hours. Don't let it drag on.

Choose the Right Place

The place needs to be free of distractions, such as the phone or children. You may have to leave the house for a short time to accomplish your resolution. A nearby coffee shop may be a good site.

Step 2— Establish Ground Rules

Agree upon ground rules the very first time you use these seven steps. Then at each of your peace conferences, abide by them. Doing this will help prevent what happens when young boys play street football. That's when they argue and change the rules after every play to help them come out on top. Our rules fall into three categories.

No Condemning

We don't do any name-calling such as, "Look, Blondie," or "You're so thick-headed." We also agree that there will be no yelling, for the one yelling the loudest usually makes the least sense. We also don't make any offhanded remarks threatening divorce, not even in a humorous vein. There's nothing funny about divorce. We don't want to plant a seed that could germinate. Gal. 5:15 says, "If you keep on biting and devouring each other, watch out or you will be destroyed by each other."

No Condescending

Watch your uses of "always" and "never." We all tend to spew them out so easily. They only beg for rebuttal, since it's unlikely that a mate "always" or "never" does a given thing. Avoid put-down jabs at each other such as "I'd like you to wash the dishes after dinner—if you can possibly drag yourself away from the TV where you've been sitting for the last 100 straight hours."

Be careful of derogatory remarks about the in-laws or other relatives. Isn't it amazing how they get dragged into your conflict, especially when you feel you're losing the battle—as if they're your reserve artillery?

No Confusing

Yvonne often complains that men don't know how to have an argument. Why? Because they stick to one issue. Obviously a little female humor, but actually that's what we've decided to do—stick to one issue and *only* one issue at a time. Too often couples bring up unrelated topics like "I can't believe you ran out of gas again. You never plan well—and you know something else? You need to take a cooking class." What? Where did that last part come from?

Also, don't dig up bones from the past, such as saying, "Yeah, well I remember 12 years ago on our fifth anniversary that you . . ." Let it go. Phil. 3:13 states it well: "Forgetting what is behind and straining toward what is ahead." Once buried, leave the bones there.

Step 3— Pray Together

Now that the ground rules are established, step number three brings you together and humbly submits your wills to God. He is the best arbitrator in helping couples seek His best solution. We're promised in James 1:5 that He will give all His children wisdom to solve their problems: "If any of you lacks wisdom, he should ask God, who gives generously to all without finding fault, and it will be given to him." We just need to ask.

This step is powerful because it helps keep our focus correct—the truth that we're a team, standing united against the problem instead of being divided by the problem.

Our physical position when we pray together is important to us. We sit in chairs facing each other or sit in the kitchen at our round table. That way we look at each other. When we pray, Bob feels strongly that we need to hold each other's hands. He feels that it's hard to stay emotionally detached when you're holding hands in prayer.

Yvonne: *Because I'm still carrying an "I want to win" attitude inside me, Bob doesn't get a whole hand, but only my little finger to start with, and just the tip of it too.*

Bob: *It sure looks weird holding onto the tip of her little pinky, but it's a start. It's great to see what God is doing to change her strong will as we pray. Before too long I get more of her hand, then pretty soon all of it. Inside me it's as if I'm having a military prayer: "God, now that I have her little finger, I feel that I've established a beachhead. Now help me to break out of the perimeter and have the next finger, and now help to occupy the entire land mass."*

Yvonne: *While Bob is doing the "military" thing, God is changing my "me versus you" attitude to "us versus the problem." God is helping me see that instead of competing with one another, we are to bring our combined resources together to combat the problem.*

Step 4— Define the Problem

Next, define the problem. That's so obvious that you can almost hear someone say, "That's a given." But too often we deal with the symptoms and not the real problem. We deal with the smoke rather than the fire.

Example: A married couple named Jerry and Susie have three little ones under the age of six. The husband has a high-pressure sales job. When he gets home he wants peace and quiet. The wife, who has been home all day with the three kids, wants his help with their children plus some stimulating adult conversation since she's been speaking "preschool-ese" all day. A pattern has developed night after night. When Jerry arrives, he immediately withdraws to his computer. Susie then gets angry, and an argument occurs. Finally they decided to solve this hassle. They had to define the problem. Susie defined it this way: "The problem is that he's selfish and doesn't think about my needs." Jerry stated it like this: "The problem is that she nags me all the time, so I try to escape."

Now both of these comments may be true and need to be dealt with, but what they've expressed is not the problem. The problem is the different views each has on how the time should be spent in the evening hours. See how important it is to define the problem? Otherwise you'll just be putting a bandage over the symptoms and not finding a cure for the actual problem.

You have a choice at this point in the conflict resolution to either fix the problem or fix the blame. To help you fix the problem, we would like to suggest utilizing what we call our "five-minute rule." Whichever one of you puts your hands up first, expressing the "time-out" signal, gets to speak for five uninterrupted minutes. During this time, explain why the situation matters to you. Have you noticed that some things matter to you a whole lot, but they may not matter to your mate? And he or she is wondering why you're getting so uptight about it!

While one mate is speaking for five minutes, the other mate needs to be really tuned in. Incorporate some of the communication techniques taught in the previous chapter. The object of the one spouse listening is to do what author Steven Covey writes about in his book *The Seven Habits of Highly Effective People*. He suggests, "Seek first to understand, then to be understood." It's amazing what this can do for your problem solving when you both feel you have been able to tell your side of the story and you know you've been heard.

Step 5—Brainstorm Ideas

At this stage you want to lay a number of different ideas out on the table. The more the better, so you'll have a number of options to choose from. As you get used to doing this, you'll find there are more ways than one to solve a problem. The goal is to find the one that will work for both of you.

Make sure you both agree that no idea is considered foolish or wrong—otherwise it will hamper the brainstorming process. That means that when your mate has tossed an idea onto the table, don't immediately tell him or her why it won't work. It would be a good idea to give it some thought and prayer before turning thumbs down.

Yvonne: *I used to do this to Bob (telling him his ideas wouldn't work). It caused him to become so frustrated that he finally stopped coming up with ideas. I then wondered why he wasn't giving input into solving problems. For a long time I didn't realize it was because of what I was doing.*

Learn to explain rather than complain when brainstorming. Too often we fall into complaining: "You never help with the kids." The mate hears this, ears are turned off, defenses go up, and an argument roars into action. Instead, explain what you would like, and be specific: "I'd appreciate it if you would help me with the kids and put them to bed at night." We're taught in Prov. 15:7, "The lips of the wise spread knowledge."

Keep in mind that pride is what causes you to assume it is your mate who is responsible for your conflict. Prov. 13:10 says, "Pride only breeds quarrels, but wisdom is found in those who take advice." Ask yourself and ask the Lord, "What have I done to contribute to this problem, and what can I do to change?" This helps you find a solution.

Jerry and Susie did this, and they discovered they had each contributed to their problem. Jerry said, "I didn't realize what it was like to be home with three kids all day and that Susie needed a break. My disappearing act made her feel as if I didn't care."

Susie responded with "I know Jerry works hard, but I never realized how drained he was when he walked in the door. When all of us pounced on him as he walked through the door, I didn't realize he felt like putting his body into rewind and heading back for the car."

The brainstorming session can be summed up by what former United States Senate chaplain Peter Marshall said: "Lord, when we are wrong, make us willing to change, and when we are right, make us easy to live with."

Step 6 – Develop a Plan

So you have a number of ideas on the table before you. Next is to pick the best option for both of you. Focus on the one that is best for the marriage, not necessarily the best one for you. In other words, look for a win-win solution. We have often written down our agreement so there aren't any misunderstandings because of verbal translations.

Jerry and Susie came up with a plan. They agreed that when Jerry came home he would greet Susie and the kids, but after a short while he would have 30 minutes to himself while Susie fixed dinner. After dinner he would play with the children and then put them to bed while Susie had some time to herself. When the kids were in bed, then the two of them would spend the rest of the evening together until they went to bed.

They decided to try the plan for a week and then evaluate it. The reason for the evaluation is to make sure it's working. If not, modify the plan. A lot of times we found our plans needed little or no modification. But there have been occasions when our solution didn't click, so we took another one of our brainstorming ideas and tried it.

Please keep in mind that if the two of you are unable to reach an agreement, ask someone for counsel. That person could be your pastor, a counselor, or a close trusted friend. Because that third person is not directly involved in the situation, he or she often sees options the two of you may not see.

Step 7 – Close the Issue

A great way to bring the issue to a close is with an apology. If you have a hard time with this, you may want to sit in a "sorry chair." In southern Wisconsin there's a tourist attraction called "Little Norway," a 100-year-old farm settlement. In the master bedroom of the farmhouse is an unusual piece of furniture called the "sorry chair." It's a small, low seat of hardwood barely big enough for two people to sit on a portion of it. When the couple of the home would get mad at each other, they retreated to their bedroom and had to sit together on that uncomfortable chair until they both said, "I'm sorry." Being so close, it was hard to stay emotionally alienated very long.

It's amazing how heartening the words "I'm sorry" or "I was wrong" can be. We encourage you to say "sorry" and "wrong," and don't forget "Please forgive me."

What we really need to do is to readily forgive each other, since forgiveness is the oil that lubricates the friction. Col. 3:13 says, "Forgive whatever grievances you may have against one another. Forgive as the Lord forgave you."

When forgiveness has been extended and accepted, then move on. It's like a sign we saw: "Remember to forget."

The final bond is praying together, thanking God for His guidance.

Making conflict work for you creates an environment of teamwork and satisfaction within the marriage as you work to solve a problem instead of always trying to *fix* each other. We think Ogden Nash sums up this subject so well in the following poem:

> *To keep your marriage brimming,*
> *With love in the loving cup,*
> *Whenever you're wrong, admit it;*
> *Whenever you're right, shut up.*

Team-Building Questions

1. Which animal best represents your conflict tactics?
   _____ The dove
   _____ The hawk
   _____ The owl
   _____ The ostrich
2. Has it been effective? If not, why not? Talk with your mate about your tactics and how it feels when you use them.
3. How did your father express anger? What did he say or do? How did your mother express anger? What did she say or do? Which parent are you like? How did the way he or she handled anger affect you?
4. What effect does the way you handle anger have on your family? Ask your mate how your anger has affected him or her.

TEAM-BUILDING ACTION STEPS

This exercise will help you put your finger on those issues that cause conflict in your relationship. Rate how you're dealing with them right now. Have your mate do the same thing.

	Usually Agree	Sometimes Agree	Usually Disagree
Finances	_____	_____	_____
Child-rearing procedures	_____	_____	_____
Demonstration of affection	_____	_____	_____
Sleep habits	_____	_____	_____
Sexual relations	_____	_____	_____
Career decisions	_____	_____	_____
Amount of time together	_____	_____	_____
Major decisions	_____	_____	_____
Household tasks	_____	_____	_____
Dealing with relatives	_____	_____	_____
Leisure-time activities	_____	_____	_____
Friends	_____	_____	_____

Talk about those areas you found where you usually disagree. Discuss ways to solve them by using the seven steps we suggested. If you found more than one, don't try to fix all of them at once. Just start with one and work together on resolving it before you go to the next one.

Next discuss what issues may become troublesome in the future and what you can do to calm the conflict before it occurs.

Father, when my mate and I have a conflict,
help me to keep in mind that it isn't
the two of us against each other, but it's the
two of us against the problem.
In Jesus' name. Amen.

Building Block No. 4

Spiritual Growth

10

It Takes Three to Make a Championship Marriage

TEAM BUILDING THROUGH GROWING TOGETHER SPIRITUALLY

Successful marriage is always a triangle:
a man, a woman, and God.
—Cecil Myers

Several years ago we were ready to start speaking at a weekend marriage retreat. The pastor was introducing us to the crowd, and we were standing outside the room. The pastor waxed eloquent on a "deeply committed husband-and-wife team who will share principles that will certainly change your life"—but while his words were flowing, we were in the midst of a major argument that had just broken out between us. Our back-and-forth discussion went something like this:

Bob: *"Quit telling me what to do."*

Yvonne: *"I'm not doing that. I'm making a recommendation."*

Bob: *"Recommendation, my eye. Look—we'll talk about it later. We're being introduced right now."*

Yvonne: *"I don't want to wait. I can't go speak with this between us."*

Bob: *"Fine. You stay here; I'm going to the podium."*

Pretty mature conversation, wasn't it?

Yvonne: *I knew it would look rather odd if I didn't go up with Bob, but I have to tell you that both of us went up with our noses and spirits out of joint. We were in no mood to teach a marriage seminar at that moment. But we pasted on our happy faces and started in.*

It was interesting to experience what was happening to us during our initial session. We were both speaking, but it was God who was speaking through us to the attendees and to us about our attitude toward each other. Fortunately, that session was a short one, so during the break time we stepped aside and talked it out. We realized who was instrumental in our fight. Can you guess? That's right—Satan, the evil one. He didn't want the Spirit of God to speak through us. He wanted to do whatever damage he could so the result would be an ineffective, powerless seminar with little or no changes in the lives of the couples who attended. We quickly and sincerely apologized to each other and to the Lord.

A Pattern of Disruption

Later that evening we talked about what happened at the beginning of our seminar. We could see a pattern of disruption that seemed to occur about every time we went somewhere to speak. We speak together at more than 40 events a year throughout the United States and Canada, and either the day before we leave or the day of the event we would either on a minor level get irritated with each other or on a major level have a big argument.

With this type of repeating pattern we could readily see it was Satan himself who wanted us slinging kitchen utensils at each other so we would be rendered ineffective. We know, however, that not everything that happens in our marriage is directly attributed to Satan's handiwork. At times it's just functioning in our natural state instead of functioning in our *super*natural state under the power of the Holy Spirit.

Yes, a lot of things we do and say come from us, but there's no doubt that Satan is a tremendous influencing factor in the life of every believer and every Christian marriage. In fact, Christian marriages are spiritual battlegrounds. How else can you explain the high divorce rate? It's sad that so many Christians don't believe there is a real entity, a real evil force, a real being known as Satan. Many think he's either mythological or a fantasy of the Bible, or they think if he *is* real he cannot affect the affairs of humanity.

Understanding Satan's Method of Operation

The proof is found in Eph. 6:12: "Our struggle is not

against flesh and blood, but against the rulers, against the authorities, against the powers of this dark world and against the spiritual forces of evil in the heavenly realms."

We Christians are *all* in a spiritual battle with Satan. He sees all of God's children as his enemy. He wants to destroy us, and one of his most vicious attacks is against Christian marriages and families. His method of operation is stated in how we personally paraphrase the first part of John 10:10: "The thief [Satan] comes to steal and kill and destroy *every Christian marriage.*" The strategy of the enemy is to destroy your marriage, just as he wants to destroy ours. We all need to be on the alert. You may be asking, "Why would Satan bother us? We're no Billy and Ruth Graham. We aren't well-known pastors. We don't speak at marriage seminars. We're just an average couple living our lives."

By attacking your marriage, Satan does two things. First, he hurts your relationship with God, and second, he hurts your testimony to those who don't believe in God. Allow us to explain further.

Satan is a master of deception. If he can get you disappointed, or worse, discouraged about your mate—you know, saying things like "How come my mate never . . . ?" or, "I know a lot of people who would appreciate me more than my mate does," thoughts like that—then the evil one has just stolen your joy. His next crafty step is to get you looking around for *a better deal*, and he makes you think that just possibly he has a better answer for your marriage than God does. Simply put, it's deception; yet look at the thousands who fall for it every year. At times the deception can be very subtle, such as through encouraging you to put all your time and energy into your children or your work and spending very little time with your mate. Or he entices you with someone else who seems to be so caring. Often when these deceptions occur in our lives, instead of drawing closer to God and seeking His help, we pull an Adam and Eve and run and hide from Him, as they did when they realized they were naked.

We know what we're doing wrong. It seems that when we're ashamed of not following God's plan, the bond between God and us is disrupted. Then hiding can become more frequent if these matters aren't dealt with through forgiveness.

Hey—Why Bother If Christian Marriages Are Failing?

Another reason the evil one goes after your marriage is because marriage is a picture of Christ's relationship with His bride, the Church (Eph. 5:25-32). If Satan can destroy Christian marriages, he can destroy Christ's testimony to unbelievers. Unbelievers will say in so many words, "Hey—if Christians live by God's principles and yet their marriages are failing, why should I bother to try any of God's principles, because they obviously won't work for me either."

We knew that God had a wonderful working plan for our marriage, just as He does for yours. That plan is found in the latter part of our paraphrased John 10:10: "I [Jesus] have come that *Christian marriages* may have life, and have it to the full." That's what happens to a marriage that is yielded to the Lord. It is a completely full life. It takes three to have a championship marriage—the Lord as the coach and the husband and wife as the team players.

We found that when we placed God at the center of our marriage it made a major difference. We especially found this out when we both lost our jobs, as we mentioned in chapter 1.

At first it was no big deal because we had a little extra money that would get us by until we were employed again. What actually happened, though, was that we could not get work anywhere—and our money was depleting fast. It was a very stressful time for both of us, especially since we had previously built up some consumer debt. These additional sums added more stress.

As the expression goes, this was now make-it-or-break-it time. During this no-work-and-no-income transition, we had the choice of being at each other's throats or drawing closer to each other. We both knew to allow God to be our coach, so instead of being a dreadful time, those days turned into a tremendous growth period for us as individuals and as a marriage team. God was so faithful. He provided for us in ways we couldn't have arranged ourselves.

We were also learning the benefit of not being in debt. In fact, it was during this time of unemployment that we started our process of getting out of debt. In His unique way, God always provided the necessary funds. He is faithful.

We were learning what Eccles. 4:12 means when it says, "A cord of three strands is not quickly broken." We felt we were starting to unravel, but God kept us together.

We implemented five important spiritual tools that helped us grow closer together during a time of stress. We call them our "togetherness tools." These are highly effective in helping deflate Satan's dirty tricks bag while at the same time helping us grow together in a way that's stronger than any bond we know.

Togetherness Tool No. 1—Growing Individually

You may think, "How does this help us grow together?" Through your prayer times and reading the Bible, you are surrendering your will to God's loving control, and in that process He is molding you into the likeness of His Son, Jesus Christ. You are changing into a better person, partner, and parent. Look at two ways this benefits your marriage.

The Lord helps you be a servant. In our natural state, our goal is personal happiness. This, then, causes us to want to control others rather than *serve* them, and that often includes your mate. If you find yourself competing to rule the roost, then you need to submit yourself to Jesus' Lordship. He turns the control into service.

The Lord helps you not to be self-centered. Without God, you and your spouse will deal with each other as two selfish people, each trying to obtain your rights. In Gal. 5:16, 19-23 we find the answer:

> Live by the Spirit, and you will not gratify the desires of the sinful nature. . . . The acts of the sinful nature are obvious: sexual immorality, impurity and debauchery; idolatry and witchcraft; hatred, discord, jealousy, fits of rage, selfish ambition, dissensions, factions and envy; drunkenness, orgies, and the like. I warn you, as I did before, that those who live like this will not inherit the kingdom of God. But the fruit of the Spirit is love, joy, peace, patience, kindness, goodness, faithfulness, gentleness and self-control. Against such things there is no law.

The selfish behaviors on this list are those that can cause major marital problems. Now look at the fruit of the Spirit, and in contrast you see that those characteristics are the things that can make your marriage strong. It builds unity to be of one mind and one heart and one life.

We can tell the difference in our attitudes when one of us has not been studying and applying God's Word, for we get a bit uptight and picky with each other. It's like the phrase we once heard: "A Bible that's falling apart usually belongs to a person who isn't."

One of us will say to the other something really subtle like, "Hmmm—haven't been in the Word lately, have you?" Yeah, right—subtle! Whichever one of us is *out of it* gets the message. We are now keenly aware that our first and most important relationship is with our Heavenly Father, and if that is neglected, then our whole being gets out of whack. Another way to put this is that we revert back to our old ways and once again live under our own limited power instead of the Holy Spirit's unlimited power.

Something that visually enabled us to understand how our individual growth helped our marriage was a picture of a trian-

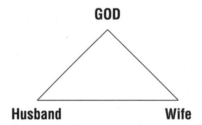

GOD

Husband   **Wife**

gle, as shown here. It shows God at the apex and the husband and wife at the other two angles.

This diagram shows that as each individual grows closer in his or her own personal relationship with God, he or she will also be growing closer to the other.

Togetherness Tool No. 2—
Prayer for Your Mate

Do you ever consider that it's a *privilege* to lift your mate up in prayer before our Lord? What an *honor* to ask Him to guide, comfort, teach, inspire, bless, and protect your mate throughout the day! James 5:16 says, "The prayer of a righteous man is powerful and effective." Knowing this spiritual reality, we have made a commitment to our Lord and to each other to pray daily for each other.

When we talk about praying for your mate, some couples want to know more about it. "We want to make sure we're praying right things for our spouse, but how do you know if they're the right things?" Good question. There are three things we do to make sure we're in sync with what God desires for us.

1. Observe

We can easily learn our spouse's strengths and weaknesses simply by observing. Listen to your spouse. Become aware of areas of struggle and concerns expressed often. Study your spouse. Get to know his or her *needs.*

2. Ask

Why should you ask when you're already observing?

Yvonne: *I never used to ask Bob. I figured I knew all that he needed for me to pray for him, but I was caught off base many times. I now combine observing with asking, "Honey, what can I pray about for you today?"*

Bob: *It's special to both of us knowing that throughout the day, whether we're together or separated, that I'm praying for Yvonne and she's praying for me. I have a life partner who helps shoulder my concerns because we're working together for the same goal.*

3. Pray Scripture

By praying scripture, you know for sure you're praying God's will for your mate. There are several ways to do this. You can personally select a variety of verses and pray them, or you can use resources with verses listed under different headings. At the end of this chapter are some verses to use for praying scripture. Here's an example of what it's like: Take Rom. 8:25— "If we hope for what we do not yet have, we wait for it patiently." We take that verse and rephrase parts of it into our own words: "I pray that my mate's hope will be in You as he [or she] waits for something not seen, and please help him [or her] persevere in that hope."

Now it's your turn. Look at the verses at the end of this chapter and pick one. Start today.

Judy, a married woman in her middle 20s, wrote us about a year after attending one of our marriage seminars. She said, "Until you mentioned praying for your mate, I had never thought about it. I started doing it right away, and it's been amazing to see what God has been doing in my husband's life. He has been growing in some areas I really wanted him to, and I didn't even have to say anything to him. God did the changing. I've found it has also encouraged my husband when he knows I'm praying daily for him."

By praying specifically, you're helping your mate become all that God intends. Keep in mind, as you pray, that God is going to answer prayers the way He knows is best for your mate, and for you, and all in His perfect timing.

Togetherness Tool No. 3— Prayer "with" Your Mate

"Nothing seems to be going right this week. The computer has a bad attitude and just ate some of my files, and the document I need hasn't arrived yet in the mail. I feel so discouraged. I don't think I am ever going to complete this project." That was a recent conversation Yvonne had with Bob.

Bob: *I listened to her and then took her hands and prayed with her.*

Yvonne: *That helped me to settle down as well as encourage me. I didn't feel I was struggling all alone but that my husband and the Lord were teaming up to help me.*

We have found that many Christian couples don't know the wonderful benefits to their marriage that praying together will impart. It's one of the strongest blessings they can receive. At our seminars when we ask couples who pray together on a regular basis to raise their hands, it's usually only 10 to 15 percent—a very small percentage of the group.

Why Pray Together?

What a powerful tool prayer is for the believer and follower of Christ. It is certainly powerful in our lives. Following are three benefits of praying that we recommend to all Christian couples:

1. Praying together reminds us that God is in control of everything. We become aware of God's presence because we

know that when we pray together, God is in our midst to guide and direct us in the day-to-day workings of our marriage. Jesus said in Matt. 18:19-20, "I tell you that if two of you on earth agree about anything you ask for, it will be done for you by my Father in heaven. For where two or three come together in my name, there am I with them." Remember that the function of prayer is to place God at the center of our attention.

2. Praying together allows us to share one another's burdens. Shared burdens become lighter burdens. The Lord knows that when we keep the problems of life to ourselves, life seems to be pressing down harder. That's why Paul instructed us in Gal. 6:2 to "carry each other's burdens." It helps everyone gain a proper perspective on problems and not feel alone.

3. Praying together helps us gain God's protection. As we mentioned earlier, attacks from the enemy are going to occur. Satan and his demonic forces do not want any Christian marriage to succeed. But be of good cheer as you look at God's promises in 2 Thess. 3:3: "The Lord is faithful, and he will strengthen and protect you from the evil one."

Excuses for Not Praying

Knowing this information, however, and putting it into practice can be two different ball games. Maybe you're now where we were once. We had too many excuses as to why we couldn't pray together. Often one of the issues couples wrestle with is vulnerability. It can be scary to open up yourself fully to your mate while talking with the Heavenly Father. Instead of correctly handling this, we decided to play what is known as the "cheap shot" game. Hidden in the guise of prayer was really a sneaky message to our spouse, since we weren't honest enough to personally confront each other with it. Examples:

Yvonne: *Lord, please help Bob to see the many errors of his way.*

Bob: *Dear Lord, you know how much Yvonne struggles with her big mouth. Help her to see that every time she opens it up all she does is exchange feet.*

We were constantly trying to get a message *to* each other as well as *at* each other, because we certainly weren't talking to God.

Another excuse dealt with accountability. If we prayed about an area of our life that needed work, or if we admitted a mistake, we knew that our mate would be watching to see what the other would do. We both thought it would be so much easier to deal with these matters alone with God. Frankly, we feared accountability, yet we all need it, and who better to help us than our mate?

When we say "accountability," we don't mean we play the role of Holy Spirit and try to convict each other. What we do mean is that we will be there to help and support each other in areas that need attention.

A Pastor's New Prayer Life

A pastor with his wife of nearly 30 years came to us during a break at a pastors' and spouses' conference where we were speaking. He told us that he and his wife had heard us speak six months before at his denominational couples' retreat. He said, "When I heard you talk about praying together as a husband and wife, my heart felt as if it had been pierced with an arrow. As a pastor, I would pray when I gave a sermon or taught classes. I would pray with individuals during counseling sessions. But in all our years of marriage, I never prayed with my wife. It was partly due to the fact that each of us had our own individual devotional and prayer times, and I felt that was enough. But another reason I didn't want to confront this was fear. I realized I was afraid to be vulnerable before my own wife. I knew that if I prayed openly with her, then she would know all my struggles and maybe even hold me accountable in areas I needed to change. However, your enthusiasm for what it has done in your lives was catching. I realized there were parts of my life I had never allowed my wife into, and it was preventing us from truly feeling close. I wanted a change; and in six months of praying together I have experienced many changes. It's too bad it took me so many years to figure this out. I thank you for allowing God to speak through you to minister to this minister."

Possibly the fear of being vulnerable or accountable is not what is stopping you from praying together. It could be you just don't know how to get started and what to do when you're together. Getting started can be uncomfortable for many people, and too often when that occurs, instead of giving it the ol' college try, they'll back off and then put it off.

Yvonne was admittedly uncomfortable with the idea of praying out loud when we first started praying together as newlyweds. Her discomfort was because she was a fairly new Christian and hadn't attended church while growing up. Bob hadn't attended church either when growing up, but he had become a Christian many years before his marriage, while working as an actor. On the location shoot, an actress who was a Christian witnessed to Bob, who then responded to her invitation to attend a college-age weekend conference. It was at the Forest Home Christian Conference Center in southern California that Bob had his *second* birth, and then he later started a ministry in Hawaii, where he became active as a national speaker and was known as "The Chaplain of Waikiki Beach." As a Christian speaker, Bob prayed out loud in public. Though Yvonne is a verbal person, when the two of us would start to pray, she would clam up.

Yvonne: *Since prayer was so new to me, I felt so inadequate expressing my thoughts out loud. I could only express my thoughts silently to the Lord.*

Bob: *I helped my beloved gain the confidence to pray out loud by encouraging her and by asking the Holy Spirit to take control of her thoughts, her expressions, and her physical abilities to speak. It was decided, when we first started this, that I would pray out loud, and Yvonne would pray along silently in agreement.*

When Yvonne finally ventured to pray out loud, she started by reading a psalm as her prayer. Eventually she "moved up" to conversational praying.

Yvonne: *I believe what helped me to open up was that we decided on two things when we prayed together. First, our times together would be short. It's the* strength *of our prayers that's more important than the* length. *Second, we would pray sentence prayers. They are single sentences; you just pray one or two of them. For example, I would say, "Thank You, Lord, for providing us with a roof over our heads." Bob could then say a sentence: "We give You thanks for the way You provided a way for us to buy a house when we didn't think we could afford one." At times we would stop there, or other times we would go back and forth with more sentence prayers. Learning to start my prayer life with sentence prayers took the pressure off me. I could relax and focus on the Lord as we were praying. Bob's patience, the Holy Spirit's prompt-*

*ings, and the sentence prayers were the three particulars that helped
me overcome my fear.*

A Tremendous Time of Closeness for Us

We encourage you to make praying together a regular part
of your daily lives. With moist eyes, Roger and Maryanne came
up to us at the end of one of our marriage retreats and said they
did something the night before that they hadn't done in many
years. Naturally, our ears perked up alongside our curiosity.
Roger said, "Yesterday, when you mentioned praying together
as a couple, I realized that I had pushed God out of my life over
the last 10 years. But last night I literally got down on my knees
and talked to God. I mean *really* talked to Him, and not just my
usual fluff from the surface. Then Maryanne knelt beside me,
we clasped hands, we cried together, took deep breaths, and the
two of us prayed together for the very first time. It was a
tremendous time of closeness for us, and a time of renewing
and cleansing. I can't describe the feelings we had. It's too bad
we've missed out on this for so many years, but we're sure
looking forward to our times together from now on."

Nearer, My God, to Thee

Our praying together has grown over the years from times
only at bedtime or meals or devotions to anytime during the
day when a need arises. We pray together spontaneously. We always bring God in on the process, whether making a family or
professional decision, in need of a creative solution, or whatever. He helps us. That's His promise.

We especially pray when we get into our car to drive on the
West Coast version of the Indianapolis 500—the southern California freeways. We first break into a chorus of "Nearer, My
God, to Thee" (just to cover our bases), and then we pray for
our safety and the safety of those around us. But our prayer,
whether in the car, on a walk, or anywhere, is always a three-
way conversation—between us and our Lord Jesus—back and
forth and in between. It has taken us years to get to where we
are today, but it all began with both of us committing ourselves
to praying together and having God knit our hearts together in
agreement with Him.

If you and your spouse haven't been praying together, you

can start today. Keep in mind that you may feel awkward at first. That's OK. Usually anything new feels that way. But keep at it. Start with bedtime tonight. Kneel beside the bed, cuddle in bed, or sit on the edge of the bed (whatever position works for you), and thank God for your day. Then each of you share one need or concern you have, and pray about it. Start with five minutes a day. It will grow naturally from there.

Togetherness Tool No. 4— Sharing the Word Together

A powerful way we encouraged each other's spiritual growth was by having devotions together. Our initial problem was finding a way to have devotions that worked for us. We recall our first attempt. Bob announced that we were going to do something as a family and to meet at the kitchen table that night at 7:00.

Yvonne: *Young Robert was living at home then, and when we saw Bob Sr. descending the staircase with several books, Bibles, and booklets, we quietly groaned and just knew we were in for a long night. Then Mr. Fearless Leader picked up book number one and started reading the Table of Contents and the Preface. Talk about a slow start for a Bible study! We knew right away that this devotional style was not for us, and before the night was over, we agreed upon something different.*

We tried a variety of things for a while, with no set way of handling devotions. Most of what we tried left us frustrated and deciding to shelve the whole idea, yet we were determined to find a way to share our devotional lives together. We realized we needed some structure concerning this area and came up with two guidelines. It answered the question for us of when to share devotional time together and how to spend the time.

The Time. We experimented with a variety of times from early morning to just before we went to bed at night. We thought of getting up earlier than our normal 6 A.M., but that didn't thrill us. Our job is on the road, and our office is in our house, so we tried the afternoons. We thought we could just stop at a certain time, but the phone constantly interrupted us. We tried it just before we went to sleep, but since both of us like to get up early, our foggy brains at night just didn't absorb anything.

We finally settled on the time just before dinner, Monday through Friday. Since we don't have any little children at home, we found that time worked for us. As Yvonne is preparing dinner, Bob will come into the kitchen and go through our daily Bible reading and discussion.

Sometimes we may continue our reading and discussion after dinner. Our goal is to do this at least five days a week, but there are times when that doesn't occur for a variety of reasons, so we get back on track as soon as we can. Since Christians are under grace, not the law, we can be flexible while trying to stay disciplined. What's the best schedule for you? You both need to pray about it and agree on it and then enjoy the shared experience.

The Design. This is the part that determined what we did when we did get together. We wanted to have some type of Scripture reading since we felt this would illicit a conversation for us on spiritual matters that we may otherwise not bring up. We also wanted to conclude with a time of prayer. Since both of us are prone to get bored easily, we decided we wanted lots of flexibility with the material we would use. Here are some of the things we've done:

One year we decided to read the *One Year Bible.* You know—the Bible that takes at least 18 months to complete. Yeah, that one. We started in the New Testament and stayed there for about 7 months. Bob would read the section for the day. Sometimes we would finish the section, sometimes not. That all depended on whether a conversation came up based on what we were reading. But one question we always asked was "How can we apply this?" We knew if we didn't apply it to our lives, more than likely we wouldn't remember it. After our reading we would pray together.

We have also used a number of couples' devotional books, reading a devotion to each other and talking about it. We have read a marriage book out loud to one another, one like what you're reading now. We've shared what we have learned at our own devotional time, or what we've heard on the radio or seen on television, or learned at a conference we've attended.

One year we memorized a different Bible verse each week. Bob selected the verse each time and typed it on two 3" x 5" file cards. Each of us would have our own file card, and we'd review the verse until it was committed to memory. We would continually review the verses, especially when we went for neighborhood walks. As you can see, we like variety. You probably do too.

As we mentioned, during our devotional time we also pray with each other. We pray the "ACTS" method, which keeps our praying together in balance. Before we followed this method, our praying was heavy with prayer request "wants" and light in every other area. That's why this method helped us get in balance.

We start with A—**adoration.** We spend time worshiping God for who He is. We've written down a list of attributes that we focus on, like creativity, love, patience, and so on. Then we go to C—**confession.** We no longer confess our sins in generalities, like "Forgive all of our sins, Lord, both known and unknown. Amen." No, we're now specific, such as "Forgive me, Lord, for the words I said to my spouse earlier. I know it was not pleasing to him [or her] and not pleasing to You. I apologize, and I claim and thank You for Your forgiveness." This is humbling but very cleansing.

Then we go to T—**thanksgiving.** We get focused on what we're thankful to the Lord for. We count our many blessings, and they are many. Then we conclude with S—**supplication.** We pray for others and then ourselves. This method has opened up our prayer life.

Togetherness Tool No. 5—Shared Ministry

As a family, we knew we needed to be a part of the local body of fellow believers and followers of Christ, so we made a commitment to attend weekly church services. Heb. 10:25 says, "Let us not give up meeting together, as some are in the habit of doing, but let us encourage one another, and all the more as you see the Day approaching." At our church we're challenged to grow spiritually, and out of church fellowship comes ministry opportunities. Depending upon your gifts, talents, and abilities, you may want to teach a Sunday School class together, serve meals to the needy, paint a widow's home that needs repair, take a mission trip, open your home to foster children, help with child care, or sing in the choir. Anyway, the list can be endless.

Ministry together through your local church or a ministry in your community is a good way to get to know your mate in a deeper way. It's a good way to grow together spiritually.

We recall a few years ago a couple who served their church as coordinators for one of our seminars. They volunteered to do it but then got a little nervous because this was out of their comfort zone—their first time working together as a team. However, through the experience they learned they could work together. The wife said, "I learned many new things about my husband. I learned about his deep concern for the couples who were going to attend. I knew he was concerned, but I didn't know how deep it really was. After the seminar, he was truly excited to see how God had worked in so many lives and was eager to help in the follow-up. This experience enriched our marriage, and I certainly have a lot more love and respect for him."

Examine and Encourage

A question that's often asked us at our marriage seminars is "What do you do when you desire to grow together spiritually but your mate doesn't really want to?" A hard and sometimes hurtful question.

Rick and Marla were young newlyweds when Rick brought this question up to us. He wanted to live out his role as the spiritual leader of the home, and he felt having devotions together would benefit their marriage. Unfortunately, Marla never seemed interested. When it came time to participate, she would at worst try to avoid it or at best impatiently wait until it was completed. Rick didn't want to force her, but he was getting discouraged and was about ready to quit trying to make it happen.

We told him that we understood what he was going through and that there were two things we did to help both of us—"examine yourself" and "encourage your mate." These two acts also help when one mate knows that the other is not growing spiritually.

Examine Yourself. 1 Cor. 11:28 speaks about how a person needs to examine himself or herself. That means that before we examine the other person, we need to start with ourselves. We need to see if any of our attitudes or actions have hindered rather than helped our mate. One way to check this out is to ask some of the following questions:

- When you share the spiritual happenings in your life, do you communicate to your mate an attitude of being better than him or her? If so, that sets up an atmosphere of competition, and your mate may figure that since he or she can't do very well, why bother?
- For every situation that comes up in your marriage, do you right away downplay your mate's thoughts and feelings and quote a bunch of scripture to him or her in a condemning way? Such as when your mate is angry, do you say, "Remember what the Bible says—'in your anger do not sin.' Are you now sinning?" You need to first listen to what your mate is saying and then, if appropriate, quote scripture for encouragement, not condemnation.
- Has your mate received criticism from you or felt embarrassed by you during prayer or devotions? Have you said, "If you're going to be serious about this venture, do it faithfully, not just when your up-and-down mood seems to be on an up."
- Have you fallen into the trap of badgering your mate? It might sound like "I know I say this to you every day, but I'm only reminding you how much you need to be in the Word." This usually gets your mate to do the opposite.

When Rick examined himself, he realized he wasn't listening to her, but instead flippantly throwing scripture at Marla for everything she was facing in life. He told us he was going to correct this right away. Now he was ready for part two.

Encourage Your Mate. You do this by first praying for your mate and this situation. God is in the business of changing hearts. When the heart changes, the mind changes too. As God is working in your mate, you can set an atmosphere that would allow your mate to respond more readily to a heart change. This is what Heb. 10:24 says to do: "Let us consider how we may spur one another on toward love and good deeds." The word "spur" means "to incite, to stimulate." That may be discovering some creative ways to do devotions together. Maybe it's rearranging schedules so your mate can attend a Bible study. Encourage each other to get involved in a women's or men's group at church. Ask the Lord to reveal to you what will work for your mate.

Rick said he would pray for Marla to be more open to the idea of devotions together. He realized he had been trying to make it like a deep Bible study, and that wasn't her level or her style—yet. He said he would make a change. We heard from them three months later, and they're both delighted about a devotional series they're having together. Keep in mind that we all grow at different rates and in different ways. That's why we need to entrust our mate to the Lord.

TEAM-BUILDING QUESTIONS

1. In what ways are you working together to develop spiritual intimacy?
   _____ Attending church together
   _____ Praying together on a regular basis
   _____ Participating in a small-group Bible study
   _____ Reading the Bible together on a regular basis
   _____ Serving together at church
   _____ Volunteering together at a parachurch ministry
   _____ Other _____
2. What areas of prayer cause you the most struggles? What specifically can you do to overcome those struggles?
3. Are you and your spouse satisfied with your current level of church involvement? If not, why? What can you do?
4. What do you think you need from your spouse to help you grow spiritually?
   _____ Help me free up more time daily to devote to prayer, Bible reading, and Bible study.
   _____ Help with child-care duties or household responsibilities so I can participate in ministry opportunities.
   _____ Other _____

TEAM-BUILDING ACTION STEPS

1. Use the following verses when you pray for your mate

Ps. 119:18	Heb. 10:38	Isa. 40:31
Ps. 119:27	Ps. 31:24	Isa. 41:17
Col. 3:15	Phil. 1:6	1 Pet. 5:7
Ps. 130:5	Phil. 4:13	1 John 4:4

2. Start a prayer log as a couple. Write down the things, events, and people you want to pray for. Pray for them. When there's an answer, write it down, so you can also focus on what God has done.

Father, thank You that every detail of my marriage
and every detail of my life concerns You.
Thank You that You want to give me direction
as I live as a teammate. In Jesus' name. Amen.

Building Block No. 5

Changes

11

The Power to Change

Team Wrap-up

*God grant me the courage to change that which should
be changed, the serenity to accept that which cannot
be changed, and the wisdom to know the difference.*
—Reinhold Niebuhr

*T*hroughout this book we've been writing about ways
you can meet the needs of your mate, whether they be communication needs, emotional needs, spiritual needs, or whatever.

Knowing your mate's needs is one ball game. Meeting
those needs can be another ball game. You may have award-
winning best intentions of wanting to meet the different needs
of your mate, but if those best intentions are not followed up
with action, your mate can become disappointed and discouraged. He or she could easily think, "There my spouse goes
again. Same old promises, but never following through."

Although you truly want to take positive actions but are
not doing so, it's more than likely that the sticking point has
something to do with changes that need to be made in *your* life.
Some may be minor. Some may be major. Either way, there *are*
changes that need to be made.

"Changes"—interesting word. Often when we suggest that
changes need to be made, we find many people have a resistance
to that word. They're actually more comfortable with their status
quo. They're like the caterpillar who watched a beautiful butterfly
flutter from leaf to leaf and then sighed, "As bad as things are
down here, you'd never get me up in that contraption!"

The problem is, if you take that attitude you'll miss out on so much that God has planned for your marriage and for your life. Harold Wilson said, "He who rejects change is the architect of decay. The only human institution which rejects progress is the cemetery."

As we hear so often, "One thing in life is constant, and that is change." Change in our lives is inevitable. Sometimes it occurs so slowly we're not even aware of it, but look back at any of your photos taken 10 or 20 years ago. You'll likely smile at the clothes and hairstyles of that era.

Change can also occur quickly, such as a sudden death in the family, an unexpected major illness, or a spouse leaving. Those changes are especially difficult since there's no gradual adjustment, plus you have to quickly learn new ways to deal with your life, which often brings on a lot of stress. The best way to make a change is by design. You say to yourself, "I know change is necessary for my growth, so I'm open to it and I'm going to look for ways to make some positive and lasting changes." Good thinking.

However, fear often holds us back from making changes, especially fear of the unknown. That type causes one to ask, "Can I really make the change?" and "What will happen to me after I change?" Robbie Glass said, "Fear has a thousand voices, a thousand reasons why, a thousand ways to bind us, but fear always lies." We need to keep in mind that God has not given us a spirit of fear, but of "power, of love and of self-discipline" (2 Tim. 1:7). That's the good news.

Our enemy, Satan, loves for us to fear, because he knows what fear does in our lives. One thing fear does is to stop us from experiencing the power of God working in our lives because we're so afraid to step out in faith and trust Him (Heb. 11:6). That causes us to remain baby Christians and not grow into maturity (Eph. 4:13). This then brings into our lives a sense of discouragement that affects all of our relationships, especially our marriage.

Don't run from change. Accept it. Make friends with it. Change is what stops you from slipping into mediocrity and hopelessness. Change brings a healthy growth into your life.

Charles Swindoll in his book *Come Before Winter* speaks about change. He writes,

When you boil life down to the nubbies, the name of the game is *change*. Those who flex with the times, refuse to be rigid, resist the mold, and reject the rut—ah, *those* are the souls distinctively used by God. To them, change is a challenge, a fresh breeze that flows through the room of routine and blows away the stale air of sameness. Stimulating and invigorating as change may be—it is never easy. Changes are especially tough when it comes to certain habits that haunt and harm us. That kind of change is excruciating—but it isn't impossible.[1]

We often think change is, if not impossible, very difficult, because when we make a deliberate change it seems as though we're making agonizingly slow progress. That happens because down deep we may tend not to want to give up control of areas that need to be changed. That becomes apparent with statements like "I *can't* change," or, "My mate and I *can't* communicate." Saying "I can't" isn't an accurate statement for us Christians, because in Luke 18:27 we're taught "What is impossible with men is possible with God."

In this concluding chapter we want to give you hope, hope that change can occur. Just look at what God promises us in Phil. 1:6: "God who began the good work within you will keep right on helping you grow in his grace until his task within you is finally finished on that day when Jesus Christ returns" (TLB).

The good news is that we *can* change. Even better news is that God will help us change. Don't try to make too many changes at once. Start with just one area. Pray and ask God what one thing He would like you to work on right now. The best results we've discovered in making changes occur by taking small steps instead of one big Olympic long-jump leap.

Yvonne: *For many years I taught nutrition and helped people change their eating habits. For most people it seemed like a monumental undertaking and too overwhelming until I broke it up for them in small steps. The main reason for small steps is the tendency to resist change. There's something about removing something we like or crave and doing so all at once that causes us to rebel. We don't want to be told we can't have it. So we battle ourselves and usually give up before the job is accomplished. Taking the small steps helps both of these factors.*

If I was helping someone reduce sugar intake, I wouldn't remove it "cold turkey," but in small portions. If that person usually added two teaspoons of sugar to a cup of coffee in the morning, I would say to add

one and a half teaspoons next time. Then in a week add just one tea-
spoon. For sugar used in baking, I would recommend decreasing the
amount in the recipe each time they cooked. When the craving for sugar
was overwhelming, I recommended munching on frozen grapes or ba-
nanas. Over a period of time, a vast amount of sugar was removed from
the person's diet. That victory was a great encouragement, so they were
then ready and eager for the next step toward better health.

Making changes in small steps is similar to climbing a ladder.
You start at the bottom with an easier step, then slowly progress
upward to the succeeding steps. By the time you reach for the last
rung on the ladder, it doesn't seem so difficult because you've already laid the groundwork with the first, easier steps.

We've found the best way to be successful in meeting a
mate's needs is to learn *new* ways of dealing with those needs.
That means a spouse may need to get rid of an old habit and
learn a new habit in its place.

Why habits? Because habits make up a large percentage of
our daily behavior. They are those behaviors we do over and
over again until they become so automatic that we aren't even
aware we're doing them.

Take for instance your drive to work. You probably take the
same route every day. After a while you aren't even consciously
thinking about it as you head toward your workplace. It's as
though your vehicle is on automatic pilot. That will account for
those times you arrive at work and can't recollect how you got
there.

It's the same way in a marriage. Let's say you make a sarcastic remark to your spouse every time he or she asks you a
question that you believe he or she should know the answer to.
Upon hearing your remark, your mate gets upset. The two of
you have undoubtedly fallen into a poor pattern of communication that has become such a habit that you aren't even aware of
doing it. You've formed a negative habit pattern. Every time the
question comes up, the same remark is made, and then a predictable reaction happens. If this is you, you can learn a new
way of dealing with your spouse so both the initiation and re-
sponsive remarks will be positive. You *can* learn a positive habit
pattern. E. Stanley Jones said, "Since habits become power,
make them work with you and not against you." This is exactly
what Eph. 4:22-32 speaks about—laying aside your old self-cen-

tered habits or destructive behavior and putting on new thoughts, words, and actions.

Yvonne: *Remember my habit of correcting and criticizing Bob just about every time he spoke? That negative habit caused Bob to almost completely stop talking to me. I knew a change in me had to occur to preserve our relationship. We're going to take you through the steps that helped me make a change.*

Help Me Change

Apology

In most cases the habit you need to change has some type of negative impact on your mate. Before you take the next step, you need to rectify that with an apology.

First, confess it to our Lord. Claim 1 John 1:9: "If we confess our sins, he is faithful and just and will forgive us our sins and purify us from all unrighteousness."

Admit you were wrong with your behavior. As we see in Ps. 51:17, God is looking for a broken, contrite heart—a heart that's broken over your sin toward God and your mate, and a heart that's repentant. Repentance is more than feeling sorry. It means changing direction. It's similar to when you're lost while driving: You recognize you're going in the wrong direction, but unless you change direction, you won't make it to where you need to go.

Next is to confess to your mate. In using our Turnbull marriage paraphrase, James 5:16 teaches us, "Confess your sins to *your spouse* and pray for *your spouse* so that you may be healed. The prayer of a righteous *spouse* is powerful and effective." State the error, and don't legitimize it with "Well, it was because you . . ." or don't minimize it with "It wasn't that bad." Simply admit to your mate that you were wrong.

Awareness

Until we become aware of our problems, we may not even realize why we're doing certain things the way we do them. It's like the woman who was fixing a roast to go into the pan and eventually into the oven. Her young daughter was watching her as she cut off both ends of the roast before she put it into the pan. To her daughter her action didn't make any sense, so she asked her mom, "Why are you cutting off both ends?"

There was a pause, and her mother replied, "I really don't know. I've just always done it this way because that's the way my mother did it." So she called her own mother and asked the same question: "Why have you always cut off both ends of the roast before you cooked it?" There was another pause, and then her mother responded, "I don't know—it's something I've always done because my mother did it."

So the grandmother decided to call *her* 97-year-old mom and make the same inquiry. When she posed the question to her, the great-grandmother responded, "I cut them off so the roast would fit into the pan!"

Look at how through the generations they just did something without really thinking it through. That's how a habit works.

Yvonne: *In my case of constantly correcting and criticizing Bob, I didn't think I did it very often. So we set up something to make me aware of it.*

Bob: *We agreed in advance then whenever I thought she was doing what we labeled "C & C" (correcting and criticizing), I would hold up my hand, give her a smile, and say "C & C." We agreed to track this habit for one week and then discuss it after that seven-day period. Well, we didn't have to wait the full seven to see if this was a habit. At the end of the third day we had mutually counted 41 times.*

Yvonne: *Ouch! I had no idea I was correcting and criticizing that frequently. I was embarrassed and pretty miffed at myself. I then asked Bob to help me break this bad habit and put a new one in its place.*

Action

After awareness occurs, then you're ready to start the process of replacing old behavior with new behavior. Ask the Lord to reveal to you what changes need to occur. Caution: Don't just try to stop old behavior without replacing it with something new and positive. Otherwise you'll just leave a vacant hole that often gets refilled with that boomerang bad behavior. Habits are persistent and don't want to leave easily. They prefer to hang around their familiar comfort zone. That's why what is needed is *re*placement, not *dis*placement. The new habit needs to be repeated. It takes lots of repetition before it's declared a new habit. Change takes time, and since God created time, He will help you with your time.

In Yvonne's case, after she became aware of how often she was guilty of "C & C," we set up a way to change her bad habit.

Bob: *We discussed this and prayed about it and came to this mutually agreed-upon plan. When she started a "C & C" I would again hold up my hand, again smile, and this time I would say in so many words, "The way I would like you to phrase what you're saying is . . . ," and I would phrase it the way I would prefer to hear it. She would then rephrase back to me what I said, but in her own words. We both kept in mind, too, in saying something to the other person how would we like it said to us.*

Yvonne: *However, at times this seemed tedious and awkward for me. So many times I wanted just to give up and go back to my old habit, because it was more comfortable than the new. When I was feeling that way, I would focus on the benefits of making this change. I would regain my partner in communication.*

Bob: *Yvonne just mentioned "partner." This is an important factor in this whole adventure of changing habits. Work together on it as teammates. You don't have to do it alone. You shouldn't. It's too hard that way. I was honored that Yvonne humbled herself to ask me to be a participant with her. Instead of her walking alone on this challenging trail, I joined her, and we walked the trail together. That's the buddy system. It's what Eccles. 4:9-10 means when it says (again in our Turnbull marriage paraphrase): 'Two are better than one. . . . If one spouse falls down, the other spouse can help him or her up. But pity the spouse who falls down and the other spouse isn't there to help him or her up!'*

Applaud

Each little victory along the trail of change needs to be applauded. Celebrate them. This helps the person in the process of change recognize that some change *has* occurred, and it also encourages continuation of the change.

Yvonne: *Bob's constant encouragement helped spur me on. Because of it, we've both seen a positive change in my word choice. We both benefit.*

Helping Your Mate Effect Change

We've briefly discussed you making changes in your life. And that's good. But the reality of marriage is that there are areas of your mate's behavior that you feel need to be changed too. Usually the question is "How do I help my spouse see that a change is needed?" Up front you need to know that you cannot change your mate. That's God's business. But we *are* able to set up an environment that is either friendly or unfriendly to changes.

An unfriendly environment is one in which we shame, blame, or complain to get someone to change. It might sound like this: "You know, if you *really* loved me, you would change." Or we use pouting, silence, withdrawing, or withholding love, sex, or attention to get the persons to change. We know from personal experience that these are ineffective methods.

But a friendly environment would be one in which you as a couple set up what we call "mutual accountability." That's when you both agree, in advance, that your lives are open before each other so that if you see something that you think needs to be addressed, you can freely bring it up, and your spouse is open to receiving it. That's a win-win environment, and a healthy arrangement, because too often we are blind to areas in which we need to change and grow. Fascinating, isn't it, that we're not blind to the areas of change needed in our mate, but we just can't see our own? *That's* why we need our mate's help.

As good as that sounds, sadly too often we close the door of our life to our mate and even place a "Do not disturb" sign on the doorknob. Then if our mate even tries to turn the handle, we get ticked off and place a padlock on the door. Slight overreaction, don't you think? When this occurs we suffer, our mate suffers, and our marriage suffers.

Bob: *For years I was closed to any suggestions from Yvonne. I would shut her out by either arguing with her or clamming up. I was overreacting for several reasons. One was the way she would address these issues. Ms. Rambo-ette would launch into me, and that would cause me to get highly defensive and resistant. Fortunately, that has changed. Another reason was that I was fearful of rejection. If she brought up anything that sounded, looked, or smelled like criticism to me, I would close the door between us. Instead of facing the fact that I needed to change, it was easier to simply close that door. Fortunately, this, too, has changed with our learning how to help each other effect positive change.*

Your marriage team benefits if you each live with an "open door" policy in your lives. That means you have a teachable spirit, not a closed one. Think about this: if you're closing out your mate, you're probably closing God out and all that He wants to teach you too. You need to be willing to hear and then be willing to examine yourself to find out what needs to be done. Heed the words of scripture in Job 6:24—"Teach me, and I will be quiet; show me where I have been wrong." And in Prov. 19:20—"Listen to advice and accept instruction, and in the end you will be wise."

Mutual accountability, when properly implemented, works, but whether or not it's effective depends upon the way we bring it up to our mate.

Recipe for Change

You'll need a number of different ingredients to help bring about change.

First Ingredient: Atmosphere in Your Marriage

Love and acceptance is the atmosphere that opens someone up for change. George, who was married for 31 years, attended one of our seminars and told us, "For over 20 years instead of setting an atmosphere of love and acceptance for my wife, I set one of judgment. I acted like a self-righteous judge when it came to things she would do. Take her smoking, for example. I would constantly read her the riot act about how unhealthful it was for her. She never got close to quitting until I backed off. Finally I stopped making her feel that my love for her was based on whether she performed in life the way *I* thought was best. I also let her know that even if she never made any changes, I would always love her. Once I matured and stopped acting like her judge and jury, she eventually came to me and said she had been thinking about quitting smoking. She's now been smoke-free for 10 years."

Trying to coerce our mate to change rarely works. That's not the way Christ brings about change to His Church. He doesn't berate or rebuke us to change. Thankfully, He is loving and forgiving and gives us the freedom to choose, even though sometimes our choices can boomerang and return to haunt us.

Reminds us of a winter story in which a man returned to

his car from shopping at a mall. He noticed a rather foul odor from under the hood. He checked the engine and found a dead cat mutilated from being caught in the fan belt. The poor creature had sought shelter from the snow and cold and didn't, of course, realize the dangers of resting on the engine block.

The man proceeded to scrape, pull, and push the remains of the cat into a plastic bag. He closed the hood, put the sack on it, and then went to wash his hands. As he was returning to get the bag to throw away, he saw a woman walk by, look suspiciously in both directions, grab the bag, and hurry off into the mall. The man laughed and thought, "This is too good to be true. I think I'll follow her."

So staying a few paces behind, he followed her into the mall to see what would happen next. She went into a restaurant and opened the bag to survey her bounty. She looked into the bag, let out a big scream, and fainted. An ambulance was called, and as she was about to be carried away, the man couldn't resist. "Hey, lady!" he shouted, "don't forget your package!" And with that he gently laid the plastic bag onto the semiconscious woman's chest as the ambulance doors were closing!

As we said, some choices do return to haunt us. Let's be careful of our choices.

It's through Christ's love and freedom that we truly see ourselves. It's then we turn to Him with a desire to ask Him to help us make adjustments in our life. We need to follow that same pattern in dealing with our mate.

Second Ingredient — Prayer

Yvonne: *As I mentioned in the chapter for wives, if there's something you feel you need to tell your mate, go to God first before you go to your mate. Through prayer He will let you know if this is something He's going to deal with directly or will allow you to administer a change to your mate by you bringing it up.*

Since prayer changes people, pray for your mate to be receptive when you get the green light. Ask yourself, "Do I concentrate more on what's wrong with my mate than on praying for him [or her] to be made right with God?"

Keep in mind, too, that prayer will also change *you*. It may be that you need to have more patience with your mate or get a different view of the situation. While all this is occurring, God will work on you, if you let Him. Ask yourself, "How do I respond when God doesn't answer the way I had expected?" Do you accept His answer or do you grumble, whine, and complain? Are you trying to see this issue from God's perspective rather than hinting that He should see it from yours?

Third Ingredient—Ask Yourself Questions

- When you married your mate, were you looking at him or her as a remake project?

If you came into your marriage with that attitude, you probably had the intention of remaking your mate for your benefit so you could live more comfortably. You need to remember that your mate is to be changed into the likeness of Christ so that he or she can become the type of person God wants him or her to be.

- Am I asking too much from my mate?

For example, let's say your mate is an extrovert and you would prefer a quiet, laid-back personality. Your spouse might be able to modify behavior in certain situations, but you can't ask for a change to a more introverted personality. Nor should you. That's just not the way the Lord created that person to be.

- Is this an issue that can be overlooked?

You may have been nicely telling your mate about a situation for a long time but nothing has changed. Maybe *you* need to change *your* perspective. We've learned that in our own home. In our neighborhood all the houses were built on anthills. For years we've battled armies of ants invading our home. We don't like it even when one lonely scout ant starts snooping around our kitchen. We've since learned how to do our part in preventing this intrusion, but we don't expend energy getting upset if a few sneak past our guard. We can live with that. We say that to say this: Ask God to help you love your mate unconditionally, even when change doesn't occur or something "sneaks" past you on occasion.

- Do you have a critical spirit toward your mate?

You may have developed a habit of dealing with your mate with this type of spirit if

you notice and keep a record of every promise broken, every wrong done

you act judgmental and self-righteous when problems
    come up

you collect ammunition for a later time when you can fire it
    at your mate

Ask God to make a change in you *before* you approach your
mate.

Fourth Ingredient—Making Requests

Tell your mate clearly and lovingly what you want changed.
Make sure you're letting him or her know that it's a behavior you
would like changed, not him or her as a person. With that approach, hopefully your spouse won't feel blamed. Also make it
clear *why* you want a change. Your spouse may not understand
why it's important to you unless you say why. Then ask for suggestions as to what you both can do to make the change happen.

Fifth Ingredient—Reinforce, Reinforce, Reinforce

Notice the change. Don't ignore it. Give your spouse words
of encouragement and praise. Those are crucial to the success of
the change, help prevent giving up, and continue the process
of change. And, for certain, take the following comments *out* of
your vocabulary: "Well, it's about time," or, "How long is this
going to last this time?" If we make remarks like that to our
mate, he or she will give up, and there will be no change. And is
that what you want?

Sixth Ingredient—Patience

Don't expect too much too soon. It's quite possible your
mate, in this process of change, will forget on occasion and revert back to old patterns. Ask again, as if it were the first time.
That means to watch your tone of voice and not to sound as if
you're complaining or are spiritually superior. Change can be a
slow process. It's often a matter of ups and downs and taking
two steps forward and one step back.

The Holy Spirit—Our Helper to Growth and Change

Jesus spoke about the Holy Spirit when He was with His
disciples at the Last Supper. It was then we learned that the

Holy Spirit—the Helper—would be the Spirit of truth and would come and live in each of us (John 14:16-17). The Holy Spirit was not just for the disciples but for *all* believers in Christ (1 Cor. 12:13). At the moment we accept Christ into our life, the Spirit of God joins with our spirit and takes residence in our lives and reproduces the life of Jesus in the believer (Acts 2:38). As we surrender to the Lordship of Christ, His Spirit enables us to grow, to become more and more like Christ (Gal. 2:20; 2 Cor. 3:18).

So how does this impact our marriage? One of the many works of the Holy Spirit is His empowerment so that we can live the life God has called us to live. We no longer have to try and crank it up ourselves in our own limited power.

Here's another example out of our own lives. We were driving a rental car and heading for a speaking engagement. We had a map of the area, plus in our rental car we had a feature called a "never lost" direction finder that talked to us.

Yvonne: *So Bob jumps in the car and hands me the map—me, the one person in our family who is directionally challenged. He says to me, "Here—find out where we're supposed to go." I told him that I didn't want this job because I don't read maps very well and we often get lost and just wind up in an argument.*

Bob: *She practically begged me just to look at the map so I could get a bird's-eye view of where we were headed. I sluffed her off, saying, "C'mon—you're an intelligent person. You can find it. You've got the map and the directional finder. No sweat."*

Yvonne: *Actually, big sweat. I was really sweating this one out. So we set out. The first thing we both noticed is that the directional finder was not working properly. No help there. Then I read the map wrong and had Bob turn left instead of right on a certain street. No help there either. We finally found the address we wanted, but the street sign said North instead of South. We had gone 15 miles in the opposite direction of where we wanted to go (which added up to 30 miles by the time we got to the right address).*

So when I told Bob what had happened, he blew up and blamed me for getting us lost. He turned around and started heading in the right direction. Ever notice when that happens in a car, both sit in silence while the male driver tries to recapture lost time on the road by going from impulse power to warp drive six? I finally turned to Bob and said, "You need to apologize to me."

Bob: *I said, "No way. It wasn't my fault."*

Silence again, and the tires were smoking.

Bob: *During this long-drawn-out silence, the Holy Spirit was dealing with me. He was planting such thoughts in my mind as "Maybe Yvonne did tell you the wrong way to turn, but you know she doesn't read maps very well and you kept insisting on giving it to her anyway, and you also didn't even bother to look at it yourself. Who's at fault here? Did you respond to her as Jesus would?" Naturally I started to argue with the Holy Spirit in my mind as I was presenting my case to Him, but again He reminded me that I had not responded in a Christlike manner to Yvonne.*

By the time we arrived at our hotel, there was a wall I had constructed between us. I knew the only way to knock down that wall was to change my attitude and apologize to Yvonne. The Holy Spirit had done His work in me. When we got into our room I mumbled, "Sorry, Hon. I was wrong. Please forgive me." Guess which part of that was the hardest for me to say? You guessed it — "I was wrong."

Yvonne: *I responded with "What did you say?"*

Bob: *So I had to speak up and repeat it all over again. When I did, the atmosphere in our marriage at that moment brightened.*

That is a sampling of the work of the Holy Spirit. He empowered Bob to do what would be pleasing to God. Never believe that the power God gives you through the Holy Spirit is something minor. Read what Eph. 1:19-20 says—"I pray that you will begin to understand how incredibly great his power is to help those who believe him. It is the same mighty power that raised Christ from the dead" (TLB). Now *that's* what we call power. And God has made this power available to each of His children as we deal with life. He gives us the power to love when we don't feel like loving. He gives us the power to hold our tongue when we want to lash out. He gives us the power to say, "I'm sorry," even when we know we weren't at fault. And He gives us the power to serve our mate when we don't feel like it.

Other works the Holy Spirit performs in our lives are guiding, teaching, and convicting us when we've done wrong. Read these powerful words in John 14:26—"The Counselor, the Holy Spirit, whom the Father will send in my name, will teach you all things and will remind you of everything I have said to you." That means the Holy Spirit will remind us of God's truth in those "moments" of life—those particular situations that occur when we desperately need to know the truth and make a change.

Yvonne: *I remember one day I was out of sorts and I started crabbing at Bob over some minor thing. I wasn't thinking the most uplifting thoughts about him. I hopped into the shower, and while I was in there the Holy Spirit brought to mind a biblical verse the two of us had just memorized. It was Phil. 4:8—"Whatever is true, whatever is noble, whatever is right, whatever is pure, whatever is lovely, whatever is admirable—if anything is excellent or praiseworthy—think about such things." I was convicted that I was not living that verse out in regard to my husband. I apologized to the Lord, dried myself off, and headed to Bob to tell him I was sorry.*

Bob: *Another time Yvonne requested I accompany her to an event she was involved in. It wasn't something that I wanted to attend, but I said yes anyway. My attitude was poor leading up to the day of the event. I was grumbling a lot about it. I was working at my computer when the Holy Spirit placed a thought in my mind: "Bob, are you loving Yvonne right now with the type of love I have for you? Are you being a servant to her, or are you wanting to have your own way?" The Holy Spirit was convicting me of the truth of the Bible, and I knew my attitude had to change toward taking Yvonne to the event. It did change, and it was a win-win deal for us and the Lord.*

The Spirit of Truth—the Holy Spirit—will reveal to us when we're not living by God's Word. He will do a recall of what has already been hidden in our hearts. Ps. 119:11 reads, "I have hidden your word in my heart that I might not sin against you." So when those moments arrive and we have His Holy Word in our hearts by reading and studying the Bible, then the Holy Spirit's power is released to convict and teach us.

Your life and marriage is missing out on so much if you don't know the Word of God. Do you want to be prosperous and successful? Of course you do. We all do. Then read, believe, and live out Josh. 1:8—"Do not let this Book of the Law depart from your mouth; meditate on it day and night, so that you may be careful to do everything written in it. Then you will be prosperous and successful."

The kicker to what we've just shared with you is this: one of the greatest awakenings in our two lives as we were experiencing the daily joy of the Holy Spirit living in us was also the *shock* that since He is living in us, then whenever one of us would make a stinging or unkind remark to the other, we were actually saying those words to God, since that's His Spirit in us. Same with you.

Are you a Christian? Is your spouse a Christian? Does the Holy Spirit live in both of you? Then think of the times we must grieve Him when we make hurtful comments to our spouse. He listens to what is said to your spouse. We may just as well approach the throne of God in heaven and shout it.

When that reality hit us, it made both of us keenly aware that what we say to our Holy Spirit-filled spouse, we've said to God as well. We now want words of blessing, encouragement, and love to come out of our mouths, minds, and hearts to each other, for that will be a blessing to both of us and to God.

To see the Holy Spirit working in our life and marriage, we need to allow God to be in control of our lives and our marriage. We need to allow Him to guide us in everything we do. We need to surrender our wills to Him and do His will.

But too often we allow someone else to control us. It could be the driver behind you, tailgating you. It could be your kids you feel are yanking your chain, so you yell at them. It could be when you strike back with unkind words to your mate. That's why it takes a moment-by-moment, daily yielding to the workings of the Holy Spirit in your life, which allows Him to work through you so you'll act toward others and not react.

When you walk in the Spirit, your life will demonstrate more and more the fruit of the Spirit, like love, joy, peace, patience, kindness, goodness, faithfulness, gentleness, and self-control. You'll also experience His power to resist temptation and sin (1 Cor. 10:13). These things will greatly help us in our journey of living as teammates.

As we have spoken about the Holy Spirit giving us the power to make a change, you may be thinking, "That sounds great, and it's something I want, but frankly, I'm not sure if I'm even a child of God. I don't know if I'm a Christian."

OK, that's an honest statement, and God loves honesty when people seek Him, so let us conclude with this. You need to realize that God loves you greatly. It's not an accident that you were born. It's not an accident that you're in the marriage you're in. It's not an accident that you're reading this book. God has a special plan for your life. That's what we're told in Jer. 29:11—"'I know the plans I have for you,' declares the LORD, 'plans to prosper you and not to harm you, plans to give you hope and a future.'"

If you're not experiencing His love and plans for you, it's because you're separated from Him by your sin. Sin—selfish independent nature—that wants to go its own way instead of God's way. Rom. 3:23 teaches us, "For all have sinned and fall short of the glory of God."

The good news for all of us is that Jesus died for our sins. Through His death on the Cross, He paid the penalty for our sins so we can have a relationship with our Creator. Rom. 5:8 says, "God demonstrates his own love for us in this: While we were still sinners, Christ died for us." All you need to do is to repent of your sins and invite Jesus Christ to come into your life. Jesus says in Rev. 3:20, "Here I am! I stand at the door and knock. If anyone hears my voice and opens the door, I will come in and eat with him, and he with me."

When you pray (talk to God) and ask Jesus Christ to come into your life, forgive your sins, and take complete control of your life, He gives you a guarantee that your sins have been forgiven (John 1:29). When you pray that prayer, you'll have power to deal with everything that comes into your life (1 Cor. 12:13), and you have His promise that you will spend eternity with Him following your physical death (John 14:2). If you've never done this before, we invite you right now to say this prayer:

> Dear God, I need You and I want You. I believe You sent Your Son, Jesus, to die for my sins so I can be forgiven. I turn away from them, and I'm sorry that I committed those sins. Right now I'm opening the door and am inviting You to come into my heart and life. I want to live the rest of my life the way You want me to, and I want to become the person You want me to be. I'm thankful, too, to know that when I die I'll spend my eternal life with You. I pray this prayer in the name of Jesus Christ. Amen.

By praying this prayer sincerely you have just become a Christian. Hallelujah! You will now begin a growing love relationship with God. This relationship will grow by your reading and obeying what is in the Bible. Talk with Him daily. That's what prayer is. And it's very important that you get involved with a local, Christ-centered church if you're not already in one. You will need to be surrounded by other Christians who will help you grow in your faith.

Welcome to the family!

Both of us believe that our Lord spoke through us as we wrote these pages, and we trust He has spoken to you as well. May the incredible adventure called a Christian marriage grow and glow in your life.

TEAM-BUILDING QUESTIONS

1. In what areas of your marriage has fear or resistance to change held you back from making a change? As you look at those areas, answer this: Which would be worse for your relationship—changing or not changing? Why?
2. What ineffective ways have you used to get your mate to change? Pouting, intimidation, criticism, blaming, or other ways? What have been the results?
3. Read Eph. 4:22-32. Identify the old habits we are to lay aside and the new ones we are to put on. Make a list of both of them. Are you living more of the new than the old?

         Old Habits   New Habits

TEAM-BUILDING ACTION STEPS

Are you open to change? Ask your mate this question: "If there was only one thing about me that you would change, what would it be?" Listen *without* defending yourself. Then discuss with your mate how this change could occur. Tell your spouse how to help you be your best. Be specific.

Father, help me to be open to change and see it
as a way to make me more like Your Son, Jesus Christ.
In His name I pray. Amen.

Notes

Chapter 2

1. Joe Tanenbaum, *Male and Female Realities* (Sugar Land, Tex.: Candle Publishing, 1989), 18.

Chapter 3

1. Tim Kimmel, *Basic Training for a Few Good Men* (Nashville: Thomas Nelson, 1997), 146.

Chapter 5

1. Ann Moir and David Jessel, *Brain Sex* (New York: Dell Publishing, 1991), 5-6.

2. Willard Harley, *His Needs, Her Needs* (Old Tappan, N.J.: Fleming Revell Co., 1986), 74.

Chapter 8

1. Alan Loy McGinnis, *The Friendship Factor* (Minneapolis: Augsburg Press, 1979), 103-4.

2. Linda Dillow, *How to Really Love Your Man* (Nashville: Thomas Nelson, 1993), 75.

Chapter 9

1. The authors acknowledge these "bird titles" from Gary Chapman and Betty Hassler, *Communication and Intimacy* (Nashville: Convention Press, 1992), 17.

Chapter 11

1. Charles Swindoll, *Come Before Winter* (Portland, Oreg.: Multnomah Press, 1985), 331.